AS

11/99

FRIENDS
OF ACPL

3 1833 03632 4165

W9-AXI-119

Jim Carrey

Titles in the People in the News series include:

PEOPLE
IN THE **NEWS**

Jim Carrey

by John F. Wukovits

Lucent Books, San Diego, CA

No part of this book may be reproduced or used in any form or by any means, electrical, mechanical, or otherwise, including, but not limited to, photocopy, recording, or any information storage and retrieval system, without prior written permission from the publisher.

Library of Congress Cataloging-in-Publication Data

Wukovits, John F., 1944–
   Jim Carrey / by John F. Wukovits.
      p. cm. — (People in the news)
   Includes bibliographical references and index.
   Summary: Discusses the life and career of the comedian who has starred in such movies as "The Mask," "Dumb and Dumber," and "The Truman Show."
   ISBN 1-56006-561-3 (lib. bdg.)
   1. Carrey, Jim, 1962–   Juvenile literature. 2. Motion picture actors and actresses—United States—Biography—Juvenile literature. [1. Carrey, Jim, 1962–   . 2. Comedians. 3. Actors and actresses.] I. Title. II. Series: People in the news (San Diego, Calif.)
PN2287.C278W85   1999
791.43'028'092—dc21
[B]   99-20366
                                                             CIP

Allen County Public Library
900 Webster Street
PO Box 2270
Fort Wayne, IN 46801-2270

Copyright © 1999 by Lucent Books, Inc.
P.O. Box 289011
San Diego, CA 92198-9011
Printed in the U.S.A.

To my daughter Julie
I am so proud

Table of Contents

Foreword

FAME AND CELEBRITY are alluring. People are drawn to those who walk in fame's spotlight, whether they are known for great accomplishments or for notorious deeds. The lives of the famous pique public interest and attract attention, perhaps because their experiences seem in some ways so different from, yet in other ways so similar to, our own.

Newspapers, magazines, and television regularly capitalize on this fascination with celebrity by running profiles of famous people. For example, television programs such as *Entertainment Tonight* devote all of their programming to stories about entertainment and entertainers. Magazines such as *People* fill their pages with stories of the private lives of famous people. Even newspapers, newsmagazines, and television news frequently delve into the lives of well-known personalities. Despite the number of articles and programs, few provide more than a superficial glimpse at their subjects.

Lucent's People in the News series offers young readers a deeper look into the lives of today's newsmakers, the influences that have shaped them, and the impact they have had in their fields of endeavor and on other people's lives. The subjects of the series hail from many disciplines and walks of life. They include authors, musicians, athletes, political leaders, entertainers, entrepreneurs, and others who have made a mark on modern life and who, in many cases, will continue to do so for years to come.

These biographies are more than factual chronicles. Each book emphasizes the contributions, accomplishments, or deeds that have brought fame or notoriety to the individual and shows how that person has influenced modern life. Authors portray their subjects in a realistic, unsentimental light. For example, Bill Gates—the cofounder and chief executive officer of the software giant Microsoft—has been instrumental in making personal computers the most vital tool of the modern age. Few dispute his business savvy, his perseverance, or his technical expertise, yet critics say he is ruthless in his dealings with competitors and driven more by his desire to maintain Microsoft's dominance in the computer industry than by an interest in furthering technology.

In these books, young readers will encounter inspiring stories about real people who achieved success despite enormous obstacles. Oprah Winfrey—the most powerful, most watched, and wealthiest woman on television today—spent the first six years of her life in the care of her grandparents while her unwed mother sought work and a better life elsewhere. Her adolescence was colored by promiscuity, pregnancy at age fourteen, rape, and sexual abuse.

Each author documents and supports his or her work with an array of primary and secondary source quotations taken from diaries, letters, speeches, and interviews. All quotes are footnoted to show readers exactly how and where biographers derive their information and provide guidance for further research. The quotations enliven the text by giving readers eyewitness views of the life and accomplishments of each person covered in the People in the News series.

In addition, each book in the series includes photographs, annotated bibliographies, timelines, and comprehensive indexes. For both the casual reader and the student researcher, the People in the News series offers insight into the lives of today's newsmakers—people who shape the way we live, work, and play in the modern age.

Introduction

"You're a Big Star Now"

O N FEBRUARY 4, 1994, Jim Carrey anxiously paced the floor of his Atlanta, Georgia, hotel suite, waiting for word of the audience reception to his first big movie, *Ace Ventura: Pet Detective.* Though his best friend, fellow Canadian comedian Wayne Flemming, sat with him, he could not settle down, for this film could either make or break his dreams of becoming a star. Carrey had slowly risen from obscurity in Toronto to opening for established comedians such as Rodney Dangerfield. He had received critical acclaim for his dramatic role in a television movie. He had gained widespread praise for his hilarious work on the Fox network's comedy show *In Living Color.* Now his ability to bring fans into theaters was being tested. "I knew it was either going to be popular or it was going to ruin my career," [1] explained Carrey.

Unable to remain in the room, Carrey and Flemming hopped into a car and drove by dozens of Atlanta movie theaters. They delighted in counting the numerous posters spread about town advertising the movie and in seeing Carrey's name in big letters on theater marquees. What most encouraged them, though, was the long line of ticket buyers they saw at each theater. It appeared that the movie, at least in Atlanta, had attracted attention.

When Carrey returned to his hotel room, he learned from his agent that most theaters had reported brisk business. The news was even better on Monday. *Ace Ventura: Pet Detective* not only led the box office that initial weekend, but it earned more money than the number two and three movies—Tom Hanks's

10

Philadelphia and Steven Spielberg's *Schindler's List*—combined. Jim Carrey had arrived.

Wayne Flemming, with whom Carrey had shared many arduous nights on the comedy club circuit and discussed hopes and dreams, turned to his longtime friend and said, "That's it—you're a big star now."[2]

A String of Successes

Carrey's momentum built with the success of his next three films. In *The Mask, Dumb and Dumber,* and *Batman Forever,* Carrey showcased an ability to make audiences howl with his impressions and physical humor—particularly the astonishing skill of twisting his face into all sorts of strange looks. Producers swamped Carrey with offers of $20 million and more to star in their movies. One producer claimed that "Nobody does what Jim does. He's got that uncanny ability to be Everyman and a crazy man. I haven't seen anything like that since Eddie Murphy first hit the screen."[3]

Jim Carrey's successful performance in The Mask *helped solidify his popularity and propel his career forward.*

Some critics compared him to silent film giants Charlie Chaplin, Buster Keaton, and Harold Lloyd, all known for the physical dexterity they put into their comedy. As one reviewer stated, Carrey "brings a tremendous amount of energy to his performance. He has a vast repertoire of impressions. And when it comes to mugging, his rubbery face puts him in a class all his own."[4]

Seemingly overnight Carrey's value increased. Moviemakers who concentrated on comedy wanted him in their projects. "It's just like the stock market," an incredulous Carrey gushed, "and I happen to be the hot stock of the moment."[5] While Microsoft, IBM, or Xerox dominated the financial center of Wall Street, in Hollywood Carrey reigned as king.

Critics Come with the Deal

Though he enjoyed fabulous success, Carrey was not without his critics. Some industry analysts and critics assailed Carrey's humor as juvenile and declared that his movies contributed to what people generally labeled "the dumbing of America." They complained that too many jokes dwelt on flatulence, bodily functions, and the toilet. They accused Carrey of making fun of native groups in *Ace Ventura: When Nature Calls* or of less intelligent people in *Dumb and Dumber*.

One movie critic typified the reaction to Jim Carrey and Jeff Daniels's portrayal of hard-luck brothers of extremely low intelligence in *Dumb and Dumber:* "In order to enjoy the pair's company, adult viewers must regress to those thrilling days of yesteryear when bodily dysfunction represented the height of hilarity."[6] *Dumb and Dumber* targeted a young audience and thus played to that group's taste, but it missed with some in the adult market.

Carrey also experienced what most successful people sooner or later endure—the jealousy of less successful colleagues. The higher Carrey rose, the more envy he attracted from those who either could never hope to attain his popularity or had lost their public allure.

Carrey's Response

Though the criticism hurt, Jim Carrey did not let it bother him. He continued his comedic work and gradually added dramatic

Jim Carrey, pictured with Dumb and Dumber *costar Jeff Daniels. The movie, targeted at a young audience, was harshly criticized by reviewers.*

roles that showed he could do more than make people laugh. Though earlier in his career he had sensitively portrayed an alcoholic son trapped in a chaotic family for a television movie— a role that, at the time, earned Carrey acclaim—many observers had forgotten that piece.

He planned to remind them that more existed to Jim Carrey than humor. His first attempt at dramatic acting in a theatrical release came in 1996's *The Cable Guy*. Because advertising for the film mentioned only Carrey's humor, Carrey's fans expected to see him play the same type of role he had played in his earlier pictures. But when they saw instead a serious, dark movie with little humor, they reacted with widespread disdain.

Carrey bounced back with films that displayed his amazing breadth of talent. *Liar, Liar* showcased him as a lawyer trying to maintain contact with his son and former wife. Although hilarious lines and scenes mark the movie, Carrey also brought a tenderness to his role that won over audiences.

He followed that success with 1998's *The Truman Show*, a dramatic film that allowed him to explore the emotions of a man who suddenly realizes his entire life has been on television. Using his own experiences as a media superstar, Carrey portrayed Truman Burbank with such realism that audiences felt his anguish and shared his exhilaration.

Jim Carrey's performance in the movie Liar, Liar *was one of his first to highlight the range of his acting ability.*

Time magazine reporter Bruce Handy wrote an article about the movie that bore the subtitle "Good night, sweet pet detective. Jim Carrey is proving he's not just another funny face." Handy concluded in the story that "The film represents his [Carrey's] first stab at Tom Hanks prestige: middlebrow respect, a possible Oscar nomination, future roles where he gets to die or have a disability."[7]

Jim Carrey has made huge gains in establishing himself as both a comedic and dramatic actor. Some observers consider him little more than a buffoon who relies on adolescent bathroom humor for laughs. But others who have looked beneath the surface see a creative artist who is willing to take risks and always challenge himself.

Carrey rose to stardom in one of the most difficult places in the nation to succeed, Hollywood, where for every triumph, hundreds of failures exist. Many hopeful actors and actresses faltered along the path to movie stardom, but Carrey sidestepped every obstacle.

His story becomes even more remarkable because he attained success while enduring some of the most anguishing personal crises that can beset an individual. Adversity—from family, friends, schoolmates, critics, and above all, himself—has dogged Carrey every step of the way, from his early years in Canada to his most recent film. Forged in the pain and hardship of this adversity, Carrey's personality and talents carried him to the pinnacle of the movie industry.

Chapter 1

"What Is It About Me That's Going to Be . . . Special?"

JAMES EUGENE CARREY was born on January 17, 1962, in Newmarket, Ontario, a suburb of Toronto, Canada. After giving birth to daughter Pat, Carrey's mother, Kathleen, had three more children in rapid succession—John, Rita, and Jim.

Father's Influence

Jim Carrey's father, Percy, loved playing saxophone with a local group and entertained hopes of becoming a professional musician, but when the responsibilities of a growing family pressed on him, he abandoned music and accepted a position as an accountant. Although he now had a steady income with which to support his family, Percy always longed to return to his music. However, he realized that his future rested with the accounting firm, and so each day he would rise, trod to his office, and labor over facts and figures instead of musical notes and tunes. His father's disappointment at not working at what he loved stayed with Jim Carrey throughout his life.

Despite disappointment over forgoing his dream, Percy remained a decent and kind person. Carrey explains that his father was "the guy who would hand you his shirt in the middle of the desert because you were getting burned—and in the meantime the blisters were swelling up on his own back. He was nice to a fault."[8] Carrey admired his father's goodness. Like Percy,

Carrey later in life wanted people to like him, but he developed a tougher skin than his father.

Another trait Carrey inherited from his father was a sense of humor. Other relatives looked forward to seeing Percy because they knew his outrageous antics and practical jokes would produce explosive laughter. "My father was nuts," states Carrey. He would do almost anything to make people laugh. According to Carrey, his father was "open, crazy, always looking for the laugh. The guy that puts a stocking cap on his head and runs up in front of your car when you're coming in the driveway, that's him."[9] As a child, Carrey watched his father with intense interest. Years later in an interview, Carrey mentioned that he often tried to emulate his father's sense of humor and his decency.

Difficult Times

Percy Carrey's antics hid from neighbors and casual acquaintances the family's darker side. Carrey's mother constantly complained of one ailment or another. "Oh, my mother had everything under the sun," says Carrey. "She was a child of alcoholics, and she had a lot of problems as far as, like, the illnesses were her medals. That's all she talked about."[10]

Kathleen relished being the object of attention and frequently warned her family that her brain was deteriorating from disease and that she might die at any moment. Eventually, the family simply accepted her complaints for what they were—attempts to be noticed. "After awhile, you just became used to

Jim Carrey attributes his desire to make people laugh and his need to be a nice guy to his father, Percy.

it," states Carrey. "We'd be at the dinner table and my mom would go, 'I have cancer,' and we'd go, 'Great, pass the salt.'"[11]

Kathleen's parents, who drank heavily, affected not only their daughter but her family as well. Carrey vividly remembers listening to his grandparents chastise Percy because he did not provide for his family in the manner they thought he should. Holidays were especially difficult for Jim Carrey because he knew he would witness another confrontation.

> My grandparents were alcoholics and my grandfather would get my dad in a corner every Christmas and tell him what a loser he was because he didn't have a job [they liked]. My father would just sit there and turn purple with anger. It was horrible for me to watch because he was such a nice man.

As soon as his grandparents left, Carrey would rush to his father and begin imitating the departed relatives. "My father would be so relieved, it was as if I pulled the pressure plug when I went into this routine."[12] Carrey, his father, and his siblings would erupt in riotous laughter and feel better for a while.

Laughter Is the Best Medicine

Carrey recognized that, in humor, he possessed a talent that could ease the tension that frequently enveloped his family. He stopped at nothing to produce laughter, and family members grew accustomed to Carrey stumbling into a room or sliding down a banister and crashing onto the living room floor. Whenever his mother suffered a severe bout with depression, Carrey tried to cheer her up by traipsing around in tap shoes or creeping into her bedroom to do impressions. "I'd be crawling around in my underwear and [doing] my praying mantis impressions and stuff like that, until she'd yell in pain, 'Get out! Get out! Get out!'"[13]

Visitors to the household understood that at any moment they became fair game for one of the Carrey practical jokes, so they learned to be on guard lest a glob of butter be smeared on their face or shaving cream sprayed into their hair. Friends invited to dinner quickly avoided asking someone to pass the food, which was likely to become the signal for a tumultuous food fight, with morsels of meat and potatoes mixing with the laughter. At Christmas, the entire family donned stockings on their heads, rushed outside wielding axes, and shocked drivers passing by with their outrageous antics. "We were the wildest family, I swear to God,"[14] asserts Carrey. Few disputed that conclusion.

The ability to make people laugh came naturally to Carrey. He loves to tell people that "Immediately from the time I hit earth, I was weird as hell."[15] Even before he was old enough to abandon his high chair, Carrey made faces, shook his body, and waved his arms to get attention, and he refused to stop until he heard laughter. His sister Pat explains that her brother "always made faces instead of eating. He'd make us laugh, and Mom would get mad because he wouldn't eat and he got really skinny."[16]

As he grew older, Carrey performed for the family and for friends, not only to lighten the mood but to gain attention. No antic or stunt would be too bizarre in his quest to be noticed.

In Ace Ventura: Pet Detective, *Carrey uses his trademark body tics and facial expressions to make people laugh.*

I used to put on all kinds of shows at home. It was sick, really sick. Every time there was a new person in the house, it was time for me to do the Jim Carrey show. I'd fall down stairs and then go back up and do it in slow motion. Stuff like that. It became nuts after a while.[17]

A Somber Edge

The strain of trying to make everyone happy, however, took its toll on the young Carrey. Parents normally assume the heaviest responsibilities to allow their children to mature, but in Carrey's case the opposite existed. The youth tried to bring calm to a stormy situation; he sought happiness amid sorrow; he brought maturity to a situation filled with immaturity. The suffocating burden would be difficult for anyone, let alone a ten-year-old.

In humor he found a way to relieve the stress of other people. To alleviate his own anxiety, he sought solitary moments when he could reflect on more serious thoughts.

Even when I was a little kid, I would try to figure out the universe. At one point, I'd cleaned out a closet in my house that was four by four inside. It had a bare light bulb, and I'd sit in there with my books and my pads of paper, and I would write songs and poetry and things like that. There's always been more to me than just wanting to make people laugh.[18]

Carrey became adept at pencil sketches and won awards at art exhibitions. Sometimes an absorbed Carrey reacted angrily if anyone interrupted him while he drew. For instance, if his mother asked him to take out the garbage while he was drawing, "I would just go insane and break everything and knock [things] off the shelves, just losing it. I was concentrating, so lost in it, it was like being in the womb."[19]

By age eight or nine Carrey discovered that he could stretch his face in ways that other people could not. He spent hours in front of his bedroom mirror practicing different facial expressions and creating voices to match the image, trying out each new version on family members. His brother and sisters never knew what their youngest sibling might be when he emerged from his room. He would come out acting like anything from a modern-day caveman to a demonic madman. Says Carrey,

> It would drive my mother crazy. She used to scare me by saying I was going to see the devil if I kept looking in the mirror and making faces like that. Which fascinated me and made me want to do it even more, of course.[20]

Carrey so enjoyed the time he spent in his room that whenever he landed in trouble for some misdeed, his parents could not rely on the standard punishment. "You couldn't send me to my room when I was bad because I had too much fun up there. To punish me, you had to send me out with the other kids."[21]

In his room, Carrey watched television comedies, particularly Dick Van Dyke, and dreamed of achieving fame. "I would lie in my bed at night, staring at the ceiling, and wonder, 'What is it about me that's going to be different, that's going to be special?'"[22] Carrey was serious enough about his future that when he was ten years old he mailed a résumé to the producers of *The Carol Burnett Show*. Although he did not receive a response, the incident illustrates how determined he was—even as a boy—to enter show business.

"It's weird. I can't imagine what it's like not to know what you want to do," Carrey says of individuals who go through life

Carrey Discovers Humor

While Jim Carrey readily used humor at home to keep everyone in a lighthearted mood, he did not at first make the connection that it might also achieve gains at school. The reticent boy remained in the background until one day on the playground, when he did a few impressions and amused the other children with humorous lines.

As Scott and Barbara Siegel write in their biography *The Jim Carrey Scrapbook*, Carrey realized he had a good thing going. "For some reason I did something where I realized I could get a reaction. That was when I broke out of my shell at school, because I really didn't have any friends or anything like that and I just kind of was going along, and then finally I did this zany thing, and all of a sudden I had tons of friends."

Carrey added that from that point on he became a performer. "I was like a ninja class clown," he said.

From a young age, shows such as The Dick Van Dyke Show *heavily influenced Carrey's decision to become a performer.*

with no clear plan. "People come out of college not knowing. I can't imagine that. It must be a horrible feeling. I knew what I wanted from the time I was a little kid."[23]

Education

Though Carrey loved the spotlight at home, he was shy around unfamiliar people. When he started school, he was unsure how to act. Instead of cracking jokes or making faces, he blended in with the crowd and remained in the background. The other students taunted the skinny Carrey by calling him Jimmy-Gene the String Bean.

At first Carrey reacted by withdrawing further. However, he gradually discovered that he could use humor to gain acceptance at school. Slowly, he started to toss out jokes or make incredible faces. In a second grade Christmas pageant at Blessed Trinity Catholic School, Carrey's portrayal of the Three Stooges produced so much laughter that the school's principal, Sister Mary Joan, fell chuckling to the floor. He topped that performance the following year with his rendition of a crazed Santa Claus.

Though he enjoyed these early onstage successes, Carrey did not have similar luck offstage until later:

> Until I was in junior high school, I didn't know how to make friends. Then I found out that the things I did at home to entertain people also cracked up everyone at school. I started acting goofy and everyone wanted to hang out with me. Acting goofy became my entire motivation for living.[24]

Carrey used his humor to open the path to acceptance.

Since he excelled in his schoolwork and normally completed his assignments before the other students, Carrey had plenty of time to crack jokes or make faces. His classmates loved his comments and actions, but they irritated some of his teachers. One instructor wrote on a school report that "Jim finishes his work first, then bothers the other students."[25]

Another teacher became so upset with Carrey's constant prattle that she issued a challenge with the hope of quieting him. "If you think you're so funny, Mr. Carrey, why don't you come up to the front of the class and try it from here?"[26] Carrey required no further prodding. Within minutes, laughter filled the room as the young comedian entertained his classmates with his hilarious routines.

When Carrey reached the seventh grade, his teacher realized the pointlessness of trying to stifle her ebullient student. She promised Carrey that if he would not disrupt her class, she would give him fifteen minutes at the end of each day to do or say whatever he wished—within limits. Carrey leapt at the opportunity. In his spare moments he scribbled notes on the day's events, on sports, or on any other topic he thought he could use in his act. Impersonations seemed to be the classmates' favorite, particularly his impressions of a dinosaur, a praying mantis, actor John Wayne, and different faculty members. More than once Carrey had to wiggle out of trouble with the principal because he inched a bit too close to insulting a teacher.

Carrey's sense of humor won a roomful of friends at school. His ability to laugh, however, would be sorely tested in the near future.

Chapter 2

"Jim Carrey—Here He Comes"

Jɪᴍ Cᴀʀʀᴇʏ ᴇxᴘᴇʀɪᴇɴᴄᴇᴅ some contentment and a great amount of insecurity during his youth. Carrey and his siblings were never sure about their parents' happiness and, by extension, their own security. An incident during Carrey's high school years shattered that precarious existence. The traumatic event practically tore apart the family, which, in Carrey's words, "just kind of went all to hell." [27]

His Father Loses His Job

When Carrey was thirteen, his father lost his job. The accounting firm for which Percy worked for thirty-five years fired him. Stunned by the loss of his job, he had no idea what to do next.

Carrey reacted like most teenagers would to such a loss—with anger. He later explained that he wondered aloud, "How can the world do this to my dad?" He knew his father had forsaken the music world to support his family, and now he could not even do that. "To first of all give up a dream, to settle for something safe, and then have that not pan out is a real double whammy," [28] says Carrey. He felt his father's anguish and wished he could do something to ease Percy's embarrassment over losing his income. In a later interview Carrey stated that his father's being fired "really broke his heart. It was hard to watch." [29] The son who had always admired his father now looked helplessly on.

Percy attempted to find work with other accounting firms, but when he failed to land a similar job because of his age, he was forced to take a janitor's position at the Titan Wheels Factory in

Scarborough, Ontario. With a reduced income, Percy had to up-root the family and move into a company-owned stone house that adjoined the factory.

Carrey Quits School

To help meet financial obligations, the Carrey children had to work at the factory. While most kids his age headed home after school, Carrey pulled on work clothes and trudged to the fac-tory, where he spent eight hours cleaning hallways and, as he said later in an interview, "scraping pubic hair off the urinals."[30]

Carrey's performance at school steadily dropped. Instead of the As and Bs he normally received, an exhausted and irritated Carrey brought home Cs and Ds. He had little patience for lis-tening to science theories or math problems when his entire world seemed to be collapsing. "I was so angry I didn't want to hear it. I slept in class because I was working in the factory for eight hours after school."[31]

His family's financial difficulties did not go unnoticed at school, either. After having been accepted by his classmates be-cause of his humor, Carrey now became the butt of jokes because he had to work after school. His English teacher at Aldershot High School in Burlington, Ontario, David Creighton, says, "He was put down so much by other kids because of the circumstances of his family. It was so sad. He'd put together these funny routines to make the kids laugh so he'd be accepted."[32]

Little seemed to work, though. Carrey's sullenness and anger kept possible friends at a distance, and his disappointing scholastic performance had few teachers rushing to his assis-tance. "I didn't have any friends because I didn't want them,"[33] Carrey stated about those trying times. He withdrew further from his classmates, as if by avoiding them he would avoid hu-miliation about his predicament.

Exhausted from double stints at school and the factory, and re-alizing that his parents needed help in providing an income, the weary Carrey decided he would drop out of school. "All I wanted was to sleep after pulling eight hours in the factory,"[34] he later said.

When Carrey informed his father, Percy reacted stoically, though the decision must have pained him. He knew his son

Jim Carrey, shown here in Ace Ventura: When Nature Calls, *used humor throughout his life to gain acceptance in society.*

wanted to leave high school only because he had been unable to keep his job. Carrey explains, "There was just one tear. That was it. It was done. He said, 'You're a man. You're sixteen. You've had to be a man. You have to make your own decision at this point.'"[35]

Carrey hated the notion of quitting high school, but instead of directing his anger toward his father, he steered it toward other people and toward work. Carrey expressed his anger in various ways.

> I was fifteen, pushing this sweeper down the . . . hallway of executive offices of people I don't respect in any way because they're, you know, oppressing my father. I'd bury my arm in the wall, then I'd go through hours of elaborate conniving to come up with an alibi of how the sweeper went insane.[36]

He also vented his frustration against ethnic groups. Canada experienced an influx of Jamaican and Indian immigrants during these years. Some Canadian citizens resented their arrival, especially if the immigrants took jobs that others desired. Carrey later admitted that, for a time, he and his family members reacted with bigotry toward those individuals who had not been born in Canada but seemed to easily locate employment and decent housing, while the Carrey family could not:

> The whole family was turning into monsters. It was the most violent period in my life. I remember pushing my cleaning cart around and I had a baseball bat on it and I was just waiting for somebody to say something so I could just dust 'em.[37]

He did not confine his hatred to the factory. Carrey and his brother broke into homes in their neighborhood, stole alcohol to get drunk, and vandalized residences and buildings. "We were maniacs,"[38] Carrey explains about this period of his family's collapse.

An Angry Time

The worst period of time in Jim Carrey's life was the years he and the rest of his family spent working for Titan Wheels. In his July 1995 article for *Rolling Stone* magazine, Fred Schruers quotes Carrey as explaining that it was "a horrendous time in my life. I hated everyone and everything. . . . I can't tell you how many times I walked down to the plant and saw my brother beating the [heck] out of a sweeping machine, you know, with a . . . sledgehammer" and swearing loudly.

Typical of people whose lives are consumed with anger yet have no immediate target on which to place the blame, the Carrey family directed its anger at other individuals. They vented their wrath at immigrant groups—particularly Jamaicans and Indians—that had recently arrived in Canada and obtained jobs. The newly arrived workers spoke a different language, ate different food, and took jobs that some native Canadians believed belonged to Canadians. Carrey later described the situation as "a race war. I got totally caught up in the middle of it. We were all so angry, I lived my life just waiting for somebody to look at me the wrong way." Carrey avoided open fistfights with his coworkers, but he did hurl a bench at one immigrant.

Fortunately for the entire family, they realized what bitter people they had become and left Titan Wheels. The horrific time ended.

His resentment and that of the other Carrey family members grew every time they entered the factory, then increased when they headed home, since the stone house the family leased from Titan Wheels stood only yards from the detested factory. That factory and the rock home symbolized the anguish each family member endured during these times.

The Homeless Years

Rather than remain at the factory and intensify the bitterness that they felt, the Carreys quit Titan Wheels. The family then resided in a Volkswagen camper that they parked at various locations in the Toronto area; for a brief stint they lived in a tent pitched on Carrey's oldest sister's yard. Carrey and the rest had to make do with cramped quarters, inadequate heating, substandard food, and the stigma of being homeless, but they found a peace and happiness they had not felt in a long time. As Carrey describes,

> We were so much happier than we'd been being those people we didn't like. We didn't have a place to live, but it was like somebody lifted a . . . burden off our shoulders, and we became living, happy, laughing people again, people that had food fights every Sunday.[39]

Carrey, his siblings, and his father immediately started looking for work, but in the slow economic times jobs were hard to come by. Money trickled in from a variety of places, such as from his oldest sister and a few friends, but they were constantly battling to gather enough funds to adequately feed and clothe the group.

Carrey realized he could either allow these events to warp his personality or he could build on his experiences and construct a fruitful life. Carrey chose the latter. He had seen his father lose everything in one stunning moment, and he knew that the same could happen to him. He adopted an attitude that no matter how successful he became, he would never forget that life comes with no guarantees. "I've gone through periods where I look at street guys and I know that's me," Carrey said later. "I know how they got there."[40] He planned to remember the experiences to harden him against complacency.

Carrey absorbed another lesson as well. His father abandoned a musical career for accounting, then that occupation turned sour. Carrey decided that if he were to endure harsh moments, at least they would come while he did something he loved. "Life offers no assurances," he explains, "so you might as well do what you're really passionate about."[41]

Carrey Heads to the Stage

At his father's urging, fifteen-year-old Carrey scheduled a stand-up performance on amateur night at a Toronto comedy club, Yuk Yuks. He and Percy labored over material for the five-minute routine, which combined comedy with impressions.

On the night of his 1977 performance, Carrey wore a yellow polyester suit because his mother argued that "This is what all the nice young boy comics wear. I know because I saw it on *Donahue* [a television talk show that was popular at the time]."[42] Because Carrey was not old enough to have a driver's license, his father drove him to his debut.

The evening could not have gone worse. Out of place in a club that catered to people in their twenties and thirties, and out of current fashion with his yellow polyester suit, Carrey barely made it to his second joke before the audience began shouting insults and

Family Togetherness

Despite hardship, the Carrey family held together, with family members helping each other through harsh years. Carrey recalls his feelings in Scott and Barbara Siegel's biography, *The Jim Carrey Scrapbook*.

"It made me mad. Seeing my dad do that kind of work just tore me up. . . . We had problems like all families, but we had a lot of love. I was extremely loved. We always felt we had each other."

The decision to abandon the security offered by their factory home posed little difficulty. Few things counted as much as family contentment. As Carrey explains, "After nearly two years of living like this, we finally said, 'This just isn't us. We don't like people anymore.' So we quit our jobs and chose poverty. We got a VW camper and went camping for eight months. One by one we got jobs and then moved back into a house.'"

yelling for him to get off the stage. The club's owner, Mark Breslin, stood to the side and in a voice loud enough for the young comedian to hear, he said that the act was "boring, totally boring."[43] Before Carrey's five minutes lapsed, Breslin bellowed, "Enough! Get off the stage!"[44] Carrey's first comic appearance ended in disaster, and he and Percy silently returned to the Volkswagen camper.

"I got booed off the stage," recalls Carrey. "I was dressed in a polyester suit that my mom told me would be a good idea, but it didn't

A young Jim Carrey was devastated after a failed first attempt at stand-up comedy.

go over so well in the hip underground world."[45] The teenager had endured many trying times in his brief life, but of all the moments, that debut stands above the rest. "I was devastated," Carrey recalls. "That evening was the most awful experience of my life."[46]

The fiasco almost ended Carrey's career before it began. Demoralized, he wondered if he was talented enough for comedy, but the specter of his father forgoing a musical career had implanted itself too deeply in his brain. He may have stepped off on the wrong foot, but it would not be the only step he took in comedy. Percy also reassured Carrey by explaining that a comedian faces thousands of people in the course of a career, and not everyone will like his act. He urged his son to create what he liked, to rely on what he knew, and the rest would take care of itself.

He Hones His Act

Carrey shook off his disastrous debut and worked harder on improving his impressions and material. Over the next four years he refined his act by working in any Toronto-area club that

In his teens, Carrey performed in many clubs throughout the city of Toronto to perfect his comedy act.

would let him in. He auditioned in one club after another, using each audition to sharpen his material. As the months passed he learned how to develop timing and stage presence and how to work a crowd. "Failure taught me that failure isn't the end unless you give up,"[47] Carrey explains.

Audiences warmed to his impersonations of musicians and movie stars—he had perfected more than one hundred—and they loved his uncanny ability to rapidly switch from one impersonation to another. Carrey could perform a routine in which Frank Sinatra, for instance, carried on a conversation with Sammy Davis Jr. or Dean Martin, and the crowd howled in delight when Carrey contorted his face to look like the figure he impersonated.

Two years after his disaster at Yuk Yuks, Carrey returned for a repeat engagement. Though Breslin doubted that the comedian had vastly improved, he allowed him another opportunity to show what he could do. When Carrey's routine earned raucous applause from the audience, Breslin knew he had seen something special. Breslin says Carrey "immediately started doing very, very well with his impressions. I can't think of very many other comics who passed through here that got so good so quickly."[48]

His reputation soared in the Toronto area, and soon Carrey's name was one of the biggest attractions on the comedy circuit. One reporter wrote that Carrey

> slew crowds with accurate, insightful impersonations of celebrities, from [actor] Bruce Dern to Cher, bringing them to life and showing all their sides, not just their familiar tics: "animating" them in the parlance of the comedy world—a skill few impressionists possess.[49]

His friend Wayne Flemming, who worked the comedy circuit with Carrey, was astonished that such a young man held so much presence. "He was just a boy, but he knew so much. I'd been in the business for years, . . . and all of a sudden I see this kid go up and just totally tear the room apart, and polished and very classy. I . . . was blown away."[50]

His meteoric rise was even more incredible because it began when Carrey still lived in his family's van. Wayne Flemming recalled driving Carrey home one night after a performance at a local club. Flemming headed down a street where the only thing in sight was an old van. When Carrey told him to stop the car, Flemming wondered what his friend was doing. Carrey pointed to the van and replied, "This is where we all sleep."[51]

In due time his father and siblings found work. Between their income and Carrey's earnings, which sometimes amounted to $40,000 for a three-night stand, the family could once again afford to rent a home.

Hollywood Beckons

So many clubs invited Carrey to appear that he never lacked for a booking. Critics claimed he could be the next Johnny Carson, and after Las Vegas showman Rodney Dangerfield caught his act in 1980, he signed Carrey to open for him on his Canadian tour. Carrey appeared to be on a fast track to stardom.

In February 1981, when Carrey was nineteen, an influential Canadian newspaper critic, Bruce Blackadar, attended one of Carrey's performances and wrote a glowing review that propelled Carrey to the forefront of Toronto comedians. Blackadar

In 1980, comedian Rodney Dangerfield asked Jim Carrey to open for his Canadian tour. The job added to Carrey's rising stardom.

gushed, "I saw a genuine star coming to life, and that happens so rarely that it's worth shouting out the news to the world. Jim Carrey—here he comes." [52]

Fellow comedians encouraged Carrey to head to Hollywood, the center of the television and film industries. Though Carrey now earned enough to live comfortably, he was driven by more than money. He wanted to be a star, not just in Canada but in the entire entertainment industry. To accomplish that, he would have to relocate to the United States. Carrey would face great risks, but he was determined not to repeat his father's mistake. He would not abandon his dream.

> I could have stayed up in Canada and made a real good living doing stand-up, but I always had people going "You're too good to stay here, you gotta go to L.A., go to L.A., go to L.A." When I finally did, it was a real hard decision, but the main thing was knowing my father, who was a really good musician, never made the move and it dwindled and faded and he became an accountant. I wasn't going to let that happen to me. [53]

Chapter 3

"Sometimes You Have to Cry Before You Laugh"

For Carrey, moving from a small Canadian town near Toronto to the entertainment center in Los Angeles was a huge change. He had to quickly adapt or face failure. During these years Carrey not only took risks to establish his career, but against the advice of friends and business associates he suddenly altered his comedy routine just as it appeared to guarantee him acceptance from audiences. Carrey exhibited a strength of character that had been forged during his childhood.

He Arrives in Hollywood

On his first day in Los Angeles, Carrey realized he had entered an alien world. After renting a room in a cheap motel in a run-down section of town, Carrey strolled about the streets and stared in fascination as a parade of prostitutes and pimps walked by.

> There were hookers all over the place, which I'd never seen before in my life. They were coming up asking me for dates, and I thought it was Sadie Hawkins Day [a high school social event in which girls ask boys to a dance]. . . . [Hollywood was] like a complete other world. It was like I had walked into some bizarre X-rated movie. It freaked me out.[54]

Carrey knew it would take him a while to find his way in Los Angeles and establish himself, but he believed that he could count on the help of fellow comedians. Whenever Los Angeles comics had appeared in Toronto, Carrey asked if he could give them a call when he arrived in Hollywood. They always said yes and offered to help him in any way they could.

However, that was not to be the case. Carrey received the same reply from every contact. After identifying himself, he would say, "Remember me? We met in Canada. I just got into town. And they'd say, 'Sorry, buddy. I just don't have room for you in my life.'"[55]

Not everyone shunned the young comic. Carrey learned that a songwriter had an extra bedroom to rent, so he packed his suitcase, checked out of the seedy motel, and walked to the apartment. Phil Roy, who was struggling to establish a career in music, felt an instant rapport with Carrey and rented him the room. The two men became close friends and maintain their bond today.

Start in Los Angeles Comedy

Carrey wasted little time before hitting the Los Angeles comedy circuit, which was a string of clubs offering young comics the chance to perform in front of live audiences. He performed at various clubs around town, where he soon won a following because of his extraordinary impressions and ability to take audience suggestions and turn them into a hilarious routine on the spot.

Comedian Joey Gaynard first spotted Carrey in 1982 at the Comedy Store, an L.A. club that showcased almost every top-notch comedian during the early to mid-1980s. Talents such as Robin Williams and David Letterman had made their debuts at the club, so Gaynard made a point of watching as many new comedians as he could.

Carrey immediately impressed Gaynard. "I remember him doing Henry Fonda and Katharine Hepburn from *On Golden Pond*, which had just come out at the time. He'd put on that fishing hat and wire-rim glasses, turn around, and he would literally be Henry Fonda."[56]

Carrey won raves for his performances. The other comedians, vying to establish themselves as Los Angeles's top comic act, watched with envy. Few could deny that the innocent-looking young man from Canada possessed talent. Another comedian,

In Hollywood, Jim Carrey's stand-up comedy act quickly brought him fame and gigs at the more popular local clubs.

Tommy Davidson, explains that "We were very critical, watched a lot of comics all the time, but he was just plain good. The first time we saw him, we were in awe of the things he could do."[57]

Popular success brought significant earnings. In Hollywood this often led performers to squander their money in an extravagant lifestyle, but Carrey did not fall into that trap. Because he knew that fame could instantly disappear, he worked harder than ever to advance his career. Many of his cohorts partied until the early morning hours and wasted their time with drugs, sex, and alcohol, but Carrey refrained from such activities. Though he enjoyed the company of young starlets, Carrey avoided the drug scene.

He continued to be the same individual who grew up near Toronto. Friendly toward associates and rival comics, Carrey simply wanted to improve his routine. Joey Gaynard mentions that Carrey was "a really nice guy. I never, ever saw him throw a . . . tantrum. And he was real humble around the other comics. We'd all go out to eat after the shows and stuff and he'd be funny, but he wasn't an overbearing [person]."[58]

Success Has Not Gone to His Head

Though Jim Carrey enjoys enormous wealth and popularity, he tries not to let it change his basic personality. He still enjoys pranks and doing the unexpected but he also tries to maintain a low-profile lifestyle. For instance, he sometimes will write the phrase "Have a good day" on $20 bills and sprinkle them on park benches or some other public spot. He never remains to see who picks them up but hopes that someone who is experiencing a particularly rough day will find one and enjoy a cheerful moment.

When he heads for the local comedy club, Carrey does not expect star treatment, either. In a June 1996 *People* magazine article, the owner of one of Los Angeles's most popular comedy clubs states, "I've seen comedians who make $100,000, and the next week they come in with a bodyguard and a limousine. When Jim comes, he just parks his car and comes in—no entourage."

Some comedians forget their roots once they achieve stardom, but Carrey frequently returns to the comedy clubs where he struggled to establish his career. He uses the opportunities to sharpen a new act or to prevent his material from getting stale. By the reaction from live

audiences, he also instant-ly knows whether his ma-terial works. As Scott and Barbara Siegel mention in their biography *The Jim Carrey Scrapbook*, Carrey claims that "The stage is where you create. Standing up in front of 3,000 peo-ple, you're forced to come up with something."

Although Jim Carrey has achieved great success, he hasn't forgotten that remaining a nice person is more important.

All the pieces seemed to be falling into place. Audiences considered him one of the top impressionists in Hollywood, and he gained the acceptance of his peers. Just when it appeared that Carrey had made it to the top, he stunned his friends and other comics by dropping his popular act. Rather than continue as an impressionist, which Carrey concluded would gain for him only limited success, Carrey decided to focus on improvisation. He was about to take another risk, one that could either establish him as one of the most imaginative talents in entertainment or prove that he could be nothing more than a popular mimic of other people.

He Changes His Act

Why did he change gears so dramatically? Friends told him he was crazy to gamble with success, and one comedian said in exasperation, "You're the king of impressions. What are you doing? You're throwing it all away!"[59]

Carrey had a simple answer: He was not satisfied with the path his career had taken. His act relied too much on impressions, which he believed was the quick road to an undistinguished career in Las Vegas lounges. He strove for far more than that, and if he were to attain the success he sought, he had to perform drastic surgery on his routines.

"I never, ever want to do something that's not creative,"[60] Carrey told *TV Guide*. Rather than be stuck with one routine because audiences enjoyed the act, he wanted to explore his talent. He felt that by depending too much on impressions of other people, he limited his career, and he feared his reputation as an impressionist would prevent him from doing anything else. Carrey was not satisfied with his accomplishments. He wanted to stretch his talent and create a more challenging act, a show with an edge. Explains Carrey,

I was putting out something that I didn't want to become known for. I wanted to be myself, to create some things that had never been done before, rather than constantly sitting waiting for the next famous person whom I could impersonate. That held nothing for me. It was a slow realization, but at one point I just said, "never again."[61]

When fellow comedians and trusted friends expressed their doubts about the overhaul, Carrey ignored them and forged ahead. Only by breaking completely from his previous work could he craft the act he wanted, one with a flair, a uniqueness. "I knew in my heart that I could do it, but the only way to prove that I could do it was to just cut it off completely for a while. I just figured, if I cut my right arm off, sooner or later I'll learn to write with my left hand."[62]

When people asked why he would give up routines that made people laugh and for which he earned thousands for a single appearance, Carrey replied, "If it doesn't make me happy, what . . . good is it? I'll have a lot of money and feel like an idiot."[63] He wanted to be judged on what he could offer audiences, not on how much money he could make. He believed that he possessed a unique talent but that he had not yet explored it with sufficient vigor. As a result, he was dissatisfied with his performance. He intended to change that.

The Struggling Comedian

Carrey took acting lessons and studied other comedians' inventive routines and timing. Each time he learned something new, he tested it before an audience.

He viewed every movie of Peter Sellers, an enormous comedic talent with a stellar sense of timing who gained fame with his portrayal of the bumbling Inspector Clouseau in the *Pink Panther* series. He purchased tapes and attended shows put on by comedian Jonathan Winters, long known and respected for his wild improvisations and crazed humor. He watched the movies of Jerry Lewis, whom he had long admired for his slapstick humor, and studied the television shows of Dick Van Dyke, whose physical humor included stumbling over stools and tripping on steps. He also loved the classic television series *The Honeymooners*, starring Jackie Gleason, who "was funny to me because he was dysfunctional. That seemed more honest and real."[64]

Carrey incorporated various features from all these individuals, then added his own unique bent to produce a fresh, if somewhat peculiar, routine. For instance, in the middle of telling a joke Carrey might suddenly collapse to the stage floor, wriggle

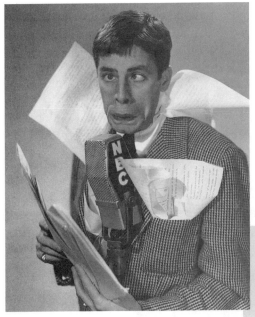

Carrey admired Jerry Lewis's slapstick humor and tried to incorporate some of Lewis's antics into his own performances.

around as though he were in tremendous pain, then launch into a routine as a deranged worm.

People in his audiences compared Carrey to a bizarre blend of the silent greats Buster Keaton and Charlie Chaplin, for the manner in which he incorporated physical humor, and to the smooth motions of dancer Fred Astaire, because of the fluidity he exhibited in moving about the stage. Though Carrey was flattered at being mentioned alongside the famous dancer, he asserted that his act was more like "Astaire on acid."[65]

To this gallery of comic stars, Carrey added one more influence from outside the realm of comedy—the underdog appeal of actor Jimmy Stewart, for whom he held great admiration. Since most people grapple with something, whether a troublesome relative or an unpaid bill, Carrey wanted to use these struggles to forge a bond with the audience.

"If you want to know my kind of hero," Carrey says, "it's Jimmy Stewart in *Mr. Smith Goes to Washington*. It's somebody who gives the regular Joe out there hope that he can take on Goliath."[66] His portrayal of average, run-of-the-mill individuals caught in unusual circumstances, such as Ace Ventura or Stanley

Carrey greatly admired Jimmy Stewart's performance in Mr. Smith Goes to Washington. *Carrey studied Stewart's calm, nice-guy demeanor and incorporated it into some of his movie roles.*

Ipkiss in *The Mask*, would become a keynote of Carrey's future film and television work.

Carrey labored for two years before he felt comfortable with his new style. When he was ready, he had to again prove himself in a town replete with talented comedians who were determined to reach the height of their profession. That determination sometimes included such harsh tactics as spreading rumors about rivals or stealing jokes. "They'll cut you down," Carrey says of his fellow comedians. "It's a tough world. If you can survive that and not hate the world and think the world is a bad place, then you've got something."[67]

At the same time that he attempted to establish a new act, Carrey also contended with his parents, whom he had supported since making a name for himself in Toronto comedy. Now that he had forsaken his early stage act to develop a fresher one, he did not have enough funds to keep funneling money home. He sent what he could, but "a couple of times it did kind of break me financially. I had to call them up and say, 'I don't know what you gotta do. Get on welfare or something, 'cause I have no more money.'"[68]

The responsibility of both making a name in Hollywood and taking care of his parents proved difficult. As far as Carrey was concerned, though, the trying times benefited him. By altering his act and studying famous comedians, he learned more about the entertainment world, about other comedians, and about himself. He realized that while adversity may hound him, he could survive. As he mentions,

> I got all my knowledge from books and my relationships with people. I got pretty savvy about things very early in my life. My fifteen years in the comedy clubs was like getting a PhD. I'd put it up against anybody's college education.[69]

Throughout his life Carrey had endured tough times. This was one more instance. But Carrey believed that the pain improved his act, for it gave him the compassion to understand other individuals and the predicaments they faced. "I don't think anybody is interesting until they've had the [stuffing] kicked out of them," claims Carrey. "The pain is there for a reason."[70]

Carrey knew that the lean years could profit him in the long run if he could only hang on and believe in his talent. As he adds, "Sometimes you have to cry before you laugh."[71]

Dreams of Success

Carrey spent a lot of time during these years dwelling on his future. He believed he possessed the talent, but he wondered if the breaks would fall his way. Until they did, he could only practice, work hard, and maintain a positive attitude.

When he could not send money home or when his comedy appearances did not fare well, a depressed Carrey would lie awake at night questioning if he had done the right thing. "You lay on your bed and the thing that you think about most is, 'What is it about me that's special or different? What's my thing?' I would struggle with that, trying to define myself."[72]

One time he wrote a check to himself in the amount of $10 million for "Acting services rendered," postdated it for Thanksgiving

1995, and placed it in his wallet as both an encouragement and a reminder that one day he would triumph. He did not sign the check because he hoped to be wealthy, but

> I wrote it as an affirmation of everything I learned. It wasn't about money. I knew if I was making that much, I'd be working with the best people on the best material. That's always been my dream. My parents taught me to believe in miracles. My life is proof that they exist.[73]

Carrey often drove up Mulholland Drive and parked where he had a clear view of Los Angeles. Staring at the sprawling city below, Carrey promised that one day he would succeed in the entertainment business and that he would be the toast of the town.

Jim Carrey, signing autographs for adoring fans, always vowed that he would become a big success.

A New Act Emerges

When Carrey returned with his new act, observers doubted the wisdom of omitting most of the impressions. Carrey planned to rely on improvisation and on the physical humor he had always possessed, such as contorting his facial muscles. As a result, no one ever knew what Carrey might do in his performance. Judd Apatow, another comedian, says that Carrey "would go onstage and ramble like a madman. Some of it was hilarious, and other parts of it wouldn't work at all, but [the performances] would be so daring or so odd that I couldn't get enough of it."[74]

Carrey loved the element of risk that improvisation brought—on any given night he might bomb, but he also might score a stunning triumph. Being onstage in front of a full crowd with no established act other than audience suggestions challenged his creativity as did no other routine. As he said, "Standing up in front of 3,000 people, you're forced to come up with something. You force yourself out on a limb that way."[75]

He captured audiences with his new act, which caused one reporter to call Carrey "a quicker-thinking, more adventurous comic with a reputation for the bizarre."[76] Nothing was too strange for Carrey. He might suddenly stop talking, fall to the floor, and crawl around like a deranged spider. He once squeezed into a baby grand piano on stage with his legs dangling out and remained there all night while the other comedians performed.

When hecklers tried to rattle him, Carrey answered with even more outrageous antics, for he refused to let anyone intimidate him. At times, he directed his words at the offending customer and subjected him to such a torrent of hilarious abuse that the crowd howled in glee as the critic quietly squirmed in his seat. As he explains, he could "either be the most entertaining person that you've ever seen or your worst enemy. I'm like a rat—when you back me into a corner, man, I . . . lunge."[77]

When his act bombed, Carrey took it hard. Apatow said that in those moments Carrey would sit on the floor after the performance, promise out loud that one day he would be on easy street, then begin crying. His close friend actor Nicolas Cage admired Carrey for his ability to get back off the floor and return to the stage again the next night, knowing that failure stared at him from close range.

He sometimes failed because he simply could not translate the ideas in his inventive mind to audiences. Comedian Rodney Dangerfield, who signed Carrey as an opening act in Las Vegas, frequently watched from offstage. In those rare times when Carrey bombed, Dangerfield told Carrey that "They [the audience] were lookin' at you like you was from another . . . planet, kid."[78]

Comedian Rodney Dangerfield offered both great encouragement and constructive criticism in the early days of Carrey's Hollywood career.

Enough of Carrey's material caught on that he eventually earned up to $200,000 per year. Joey Gaynard claims that Carrey had invented such a unique act that

> I truly believe, in twenty years, when they teach the course at UCLA, they'll say, "When we talk about slapstick, here's a guy who reinvented the form," and they'll show his films just like they do Buster Keaton and Jerry Lewis and stuff like that.[79]

Jim Carrey had not yet starred in films, but the day was fast approaching.

Chapter 4

"I Always Kind of Believed in Miracles"

ONE REASON CARREY changed his comedy routine was that he wanted to establish a career in films. To achieve this goal, Carrey followed the formula that had succeeded so far: He worked hard and trusted that his talents would take him to the top. If he got a lucky break, he would happily accept it as a reward for long hours and weary nights.

The Duck Factory

In 1982 NBC Entertainment president Brandon Tartikoff walked into the Comedy Store for an evening of laughter. By the time he left, Tartikoff had decided that Jim Carrey would be the star for a new series being developed by the network, *The Duck Factory*.

Carrey was cast as Skip Tarkenton, a cartoonist working in an animator studio. The show had live actors interacting with animated characters, which was new for television. Allan Burns, who had previously produced the classic comedy *Mary Tyler Moore*, was hired as executive producer, and NBC placed the new show in one of its choicest slots—between the popular *Cheers* and *Hill Street Blues*. Many observers predicted that *The Duck Factory* would be a huge hit for NBC.

The show debuted in 1984 to widespread publicity but never built an audience. After only thirteen episodes, the network pulled it off the air. One problem was that NBC hired Carrey, known for his unpredictable skits and wild improvisations, then ignored his unique talents by placing him in a straight role. The scripts had been written before Carrey signed on, and no one at NBC seemed quite sure how to best employ Carrey's considerable talent.

Though *The Duck Factory* failed, Carrey received acclaim for his work. Television critic Richard Hack wrote,

> To put it simply, Jim Carrey will be a star. His toplining of *The Duck Factory* . . . makes watching the program a genuine treat. There's a certain likability that Carrey adds to his scenes that could make even a funeral seem funny.[80]

The failure of his first foray into television did not set Carrey back, though others doubted he would overcome the debacle. When his friends asked him whether he believed that he had been given his shot at the big time and fluffed it, Carrey quickly replied that he knew he would bounce back. Carrey never wavered in his certainty that entertainment was his future. "I always kind of believed in miracles. Some way, something was going to pop out."[81]

Although audiences enjoyed Jim Carrey in NBC's The Duck Factory, *the show failed after only thirteen episodes.*

Small Roles in Movies

The same year of Carrey's first stab at television, his career in films began. He won small parts in seven movies over the next five years, and even though most of the movies were forgettable, they helped build his reputation in Hollywood as a solid actor. In 1984 he appeared in *Finders Keepers*, a comedy that disappeared after a short run. The next year he played Mark Kendall, a high school senior who becomes the love interest of a vampire played by actress Lauren Hutton in *Once Bitten*. Again, the movie met with disdain from critics.

Carrey began to gain a name for himself by performing small parts in many films, such as Once Bitten, *produced in 1985.*

Carrey gained acclaim with 1986's *Peggy Sue Got Married*. After a five-minute audition, the director, Francis Ford Coppola, who had filmed the masterpiece *The Godfather*, quickly signed Carrey to be one of actor Nicolas Cage's buddies. In a later audition for another film, Carrey impressed director Joel Schumacher by rapidly switching from one character to another, causing the filmmaker to claim that Carrey "was spellbinding. There was only Jim, but it was like there were twenty people in the room, all of them different characters."[82]

Schumacher knew that, because of Carrey's unpredictable style, producers would have trouble placing Carrey in the right role. Schumacher accurately concluded that Carrey "gave this dazzling performance, but it was obvious you couldn't put this guy in just anything. You had to build an entire movie around him."[83]

The proper vehicle had not yet come along, and Carrey struggled through other films. After watching Carrey impersonate him, Clint Eastwood signed the comedian for two movies. In

The Dead Pool, one of Eastwood's Dirty Harry movies, Carrey enjoyed a brief role as rock singer Johnny Shakes, who becomes a serial killer's first victim. He followed that in 1989 as a stand-up comedian in Eastwood's flop *Pink Cadillac.*

The small roles were important in establishing that Carrey could act, but the roles were slow in coming. Nicolas Cage remained a steadfast friend during these years and offered Carrey words of support. Cage recalls that he knew "it would be hard for people to cast him right off the bat, because they wouldn't know what to make of him. But I always knew that once they did, that it would be an explosion." [84]

Actor Nicolas Cage became one of Carrey's most supportive friends during Carrey's early film career.

Problem with Parents

Once money from his acting started to come in, Carrey brought his parents from Canada to live with him. Before long, however, Carrey wondered if he had done the correct thing. After working hard all day, Carrey had difficulty relaxing at home because his parents were always watching television and smoking cigarettes. As he states, "They were really lovely people, but they got caught up in thinking they were going to be taken care of."[85]

The strain of once again living with his parents proved too much for Carrey, who wanted to concentrate on his career. Every time Carrey stumbled home after a long day's work, instead of peace and quiet he encountered the demands of his mother and father. Gradually, he approached the breaking point, and at one time Carrey worried that he was actually having a nervous breakdown.

The stress caused nightmares in which he was unable to save his family from cruel fates or in which he murdered his mother. "I'd wake up in the middle of the night and think that the Devil was lying beside me. Or I'd be absolutely positive that there was something under the bed."[86] Feeling helpless and angry, Carrey sometimes sat on the floor of his room and howled at the ceiling.

> I resented them [his parents] for the responsibility of taking care of them since I was 17. I resented them because there had always been a lot of pressure on me to be the star, to save their lives, to buy them the big house with the pillars—like Elvis, you know? And it came to a head.[87]

Carrey painted and sculpted in an effort to steer his frustrations toward creative paths. In one sculpture, which represented his struggle to meet bills, Carrey's mother perilously balanced on a high wire while in each hand she clutched bags of food coupons. A frightening painting depicted his father with a gun in one hand and a stopwatch in the other. "My parents would come into the room and ask, 'What are you drawing?' It would be my dad looking at his watch with a gun in his hand. 'It's a portrait of you,' I said. 'It's called *Waiting to Die.*'"[88]

Carrey tried everything to control his feelings. He sought therapy, took the powerful drug Prozac to stabilize his unpredictable mood swings, and read every self-help book that appeared on the market. Carrey even consulted psychics until one suggested that his family suffered from an evil curse.

At the advice of his therapist, Carrey asked his parents to return to Canada in 1984. He did not want to hurt their feelings, but if he were to maintain a semblance of sanity he had to be on his own so he could focus on his entertainment career. Requesting his mother and father to leave "was the hardest thing I've ever done," explains Carrey. "But I've never had another nightmare, never had another fear."[89]

Carrey Starts a Family and a Television Comedy Career

With the departure of his parents, Carrey could again focus on his career. He also embarked on a new phase of his personal life. In one of his frequent appearances at the Comedy Store, Carrey met a pretty, twenty-six-year-old waitress, Melissa Wormer. The two fell in love and married on March 28, 1986, and the next year they gave birth to a daughter, Jane. Wormer brought a calmness to Carrey's life that had long been missing.

That calmness helped free Carrey to pursue work in television. He landed appearances on nighttime talk shows. He performed for Johnny Carson on *The Tonight Show* and brought down the house with a hilarious stint on *The Arsenio Hall Show*. After being introduced, Carrey nervously walked out from behind the curtain and stared at the audience with anxiety etched on his face. Suddenly, the crotch of his trousers turned wet. As the spot enlarged, the amount of laughter increased. Carrey had made people laugh without uttering a word.

In 1986 he auditioned for *Saturday Night Live*, a program that launched the careers of comedians Bill Murray, Dan Aykroyd, Eddie Murphy, and other notable talents. Carrey lost out to two other young comedians, Dana Carvey and Phil Hartman.

Disappointment over losing out on the *Saturday Night Live* spot did not keep Carrey from pursuing other roles—both in television and movies. A bit part in the 1989 movie *Earth Girls*

Audition for *Saturday Night Live*

One of the premier comedy shows on television over the last twenty years has been *Saturday Night Live*. Known for its outrageous skits and hilarious antics, the show has propelled many young comedians to movie fame. Dan Aykroyd, Bill Murray, Eddie Murphy, and Dana Carvey are just a few of the many comedians who owe their careers to the show.

Jim Carrey hoped to add his name to the lengthy list of performers who worked for the late night program, but he did not fare well in a 1986 audition. As he explained to Martha Sherrill, who profiled Carrey in the December 1995 issue of *Esquire* magazine, "I had an omen that I wasn't going to get that show."

As he walked toward the NBC studios in Burbank, California, he heard someone yell, "Don't do it! Don't jump!" Carrey looked up to see a person standing on the ledge threatening to commit suicide. "Suddenly, a crowd was gathering below him. Meanwhile, I've got to go inside and audition, wondering the whole time if this guy was dead or not."

A slightly rattled Carrey did his best, but the show's producers selected other comedians. "He didn't jump, and I didn't get the job."

Are Easy led to his first major television role. Playing an alien alongside comedian Damon Wayans in a spoof of 1950s' science-fiction films, Carrey impressed viewers with his physical performance. Neither man spoke lines other than an alien gibberish, but Carrey's arm gestures, facial twists, and body contortions stole most scenes. Damon Wayans, also known for the use of physical humor, engaged in a friendly competition with Carrey to see who could outperform the other. Wayans usually lost.

After watching Carrey's wild gesticulations during one scene, Wayans concluded that Carrey's outrageous antics must be based in rage. Wayans muttered to his fellow actor, "Hey, man you are one of the angriest people that I have ever seen." Carrey answered, "Yeah, I guess I've got that going for me. That's how I deal with it."[90] However, Wayans recognized a hot talent in Carrey and recommended him to his brother Keenen Ivory Wayans, who was then assembling the cast for a daring new television comedy, *In Living Color.*

Carrey's role in the movie Earth Girls Are Easy *(as the alien pictured second from left) opened up many new opportunities for him.*

In Living Color

In Living Color was an important part of Australian businessman Rupert Murdoch's attempt to create a fourth television network that would challenge the existing "big three," NBC, ABC, and CBS. In an effort to garner the big-city, African American market, Murdoch asked Keenen Ivory Wayans to develop a show whose humor stretched beyond that of *Saturday Night Live.* To give the show every chance of success, Murdoch placed it on Sundays, where his Fox network had its only two hits to date, *The Simpsons* and *Married . . . with Children.*

When Wayans offered Carrey a slot, Carrey was not very enthusiastic because he did not see much on television that excited him.

> Most of it is so insulting, so horrifying. I didn't want to be a part of anybody's sitcom. They're so terrible. I remember going to auditions and once they asked me what my likes and dislikes were on television. And I said that my dislike *was* television. And that's probably not a good thing to say in a TV audition.[91]

However, when Wayans mentioned that the program would rely mainly on audacious skits and that Carrey would enjoy freedom to develop his own characters, Carrey joined the cast. He believed that, since Fox hoped to nudge aside the other television networks, it would permit a more imaginative edge.

The show debuted on April 15, 1990, to rave reviews. Not only African Americans but young people across the nation loved characters such as Damon Wayans's Homie the Clown and Carrey's musclewoman, Vera de Milo. Carrey's most famous character was Fire Marshal Bill, a demented fireman who accidentally sets himself on fire while pointing out the hazards of fire. With each word Fire Marshal Bill utters, his face stretches and twists in a weird assortment of looks. Carrey claims the true secret to Fire Marshal Bill comes from inside. "It's an inner weirdness. It's not so much the face—anybody can do something with their face—but it's the insanity that bubbles beneath the surface that comes through."[92]

Carrey attends a script rehearsal for the show In Living Color. *He decided to join the cast of the show once he understood that he could develop his own characters and skits.*

Fire Marshal Bill and his other characters allowed Carrey to perform in ways he had never attempted onstage. In some measure they became a vent for his pent-up emotions related to his family. "I think I'm just a high-strung person," Carrey explains. "I have to spew all this stuff out."[93]

Critics claimed Carrey's crazed Fire Marshal Bill, who achieved laughs by setting things on fire, was done in poor taste and was disrespectful to firefighters. Carrey, though, disagreed, and explains that he "had cops come up and thank me. They said that ever since [the 1960s television comedy] *Car 54, Where Are You?*, cops have been raked over the coals, and finally the firemen were getting it."[94]

In Living Color offered Carrey the opportunity to use his diverse talents, including times when he was able to play dramatic roles. In preparing for a skit, Carrey fell back on the pain he had experienced earlier in life and fashioned a bond with whatever character he portrayed. "Even the nicest people in the world have pain," Carrey states. "So there's always a chink in the armor"[95] that he could exploit.

Carrey, the show's only white male cast member, meshed with the other members of the show, even though some people not associated with *In Living Color* teased him for being the "designated Caucasian." Carrey shrugged it off, although one time when a reporter from MTV asked if he minded being the only white male, Carrey answered with mock, though intentional, anger. Glaring directly into the camera he shouted, "When are we gonna get past the color of our skin, people? Let it go. . . . I thought when I came to this country, it was a melting pot. I guess I was wrong!"[96]

Other Directions

Carrey's newfound fame brought both benefits and drawbacks. He, Melissa, and Jane, moved into a new three-bedroom home in Hollywood, but now he also had to dodge fans when he stepped out in public. For example, when he took Jane trick-or-treating one Halloween, Carrey wore a mask so that people would not recognize him and ask him to do Fire Marshal Bill or some other character.

Although critics dubbed him the token white male on In Living Color, *Carrey's success on the show allowed him to pick and choose future roles.*

Carrey had arrived at a crucial juncture in his career. The television show's success could propel him in any number of directions, but he was determined to control events. Along with manager Jimmy Miller and agent Nick Stevens, Carrey meticulously planned a path they thought most likely to take him to the top. He taped a Showtime comedy special in 1991 in Toronto called *Jim Carrey's Unnatural Act,* which garnered excellent reviews and buttressed his reputation for being one of the most inventive comedians in entertainment.

With his reputation in humor secure, Carrey turned to dramatic pieces. His first major attempt to prove he could do more than comedy occurred with the March 16, 1992, presentation of Fox network's dramatic TV movie *Doing Time on Maple Drive.* Carrey had worried that his reputation might preclude his chance to land a dramatic role in the movie, but he auditioned for director Ken Olin anyway. The director had never watched

The Showtime Special

Carrey illustrated his comic diversity with the 1991 Showtime cable special *Jim Carrey's Unnatural Act*. Taped before an audience in Toronto, Carrey's one-hour performance included an array of characters, faces, body contortions, and jokes and helped advance Carrey along his dream.

As Roy Trakin mentions in his 1995 biography, *Jim Carrey Unmasked!*, Carrey poked fun at a gospel singer whose singing tested everyone's patience ("My singing made sweet Jesus run away") and at the eternally happy individual who people so hope to avoid that when they see him approaching they "would be tunneling under the street to avoid [him]."

Carrey based a significant portion of the program on his own family experience. In one skit, he recalled the irritation of having his grandparents in the same household by commenting, "Or maybe hell is just having to listen to our grandparents breathe through their noses as they eat a sandwich."

Carrey honored his idol, Jimmy Stewart, by imagining the eternally optimistic Stewart viewing a nuclear holocaust. Launching into his impression of the famed actor, Carrey said, "And the amazing thing is how something so magnificent and colorful could melt your face off."

Carrey also included a segment in which he was a television evangelist. In another routine he was Jesus on the cross yelling to the Roman soldiers below, "You guys are gonna get it. Wait until my Father hears about this."

In Living Color and did not know who Carrey was, so when he first glimpsed Carrey, Olin thought "he'd just got off the bus from Nebraska."[97]

Midway into Carrey's audition, an impressed Olin asked Carrey his name. Olin said that "I'd never have imagined he was a comedic actor. He gave a very honest reading. It was so sad. I think he understands the part personally."[98] Olin later told Carrey's manager that if he had known ahead of time about Carrey's comedy, he probably would not have considered him.

Although Fox executives doubted that a comedian could convey the proper seriousness for the role, Carrey knew he would have no difficulty. His act, though lighthearted on the surface, was anchored in a seriousness that he developed as a youth. As Carrey explains,

I think comedians are the most serious people on earth. That's how you deal with it, you know? A lot of times you're putting out concepts that aren't very acceptable. That's the trick to comedy sometimes, to be able to take harsh subjects and make them acceptable and funny to everybody.[99]

In the movie Carrey played Timothy Carter, the alcoholic son of demanding parents. The part called for sensitivity and compassion, and Carrey drew on feelings he had toward his own parents for the portrayal. The death of his mother from kidney failure shortly before filming began gave added poignancy to the role. Carrey performed so well that he, and the film, received critical acclaim. A reviewer in the *Los Angeles Times* commented that Carrey "proves his depth with a poignant portrayal of the adult alcoholic son,"[100] while *TV Guide* praised Carrey's sensitive acting as "infused with sorrow."[101]

Carrey hoped that the rave reviews for *Doing Time on Maple Drive* would lead to more dramatic parts. He intended to take whatever action necessary to keep his name in front of producers.

You've got to realize coming into this business that no one's going to take a chance on you. You have to prove you have the goods. . . . It's nothing personal. It's not like anyone goes out of his way to screw you. It's just that you have to be the most popular, talented guy in the room at the exact moment they need you.[102]

The exact moment for Carrey arrived in 1994, when he scored triumphs in three major theatrical releases. He was about to become the hottest, most talented guy in the room.

Chapter 5

"I've . . . Harnessed Spasticness"

THE THREE 1994 movies in which Carrey starred each earned over $100 million. The accomplishment propelled his name to the summit of the entertainment industry and secured his financial future. While his professional life gathered momentum, however, his personal life crumbled.

Ace Ventura: Pet Detective

Carrey's big break came with *Ace Ventura: Pet Detective*, a movie about a Miami, Florida, detective who specializes in locating missing animals. At first producers offered the role to Judd Nelson and to comedians Rick Moranis and Whoopi Goldberg, but they declined. Carrey also turned down the offer for two years because he wanted creative control over a script he felt needed drastic alterations.

Finally, after producers agreed to pay Carrey $350,000 and allow him to make changes, Carrey took the role. "I wanted to see if I could take something like this, make it into something, shove it in people's faces and say, 'Yes, this is idiotic . . . and here it is.'"[103] Over a four-month span in 1992, Carrey and partner Tom Shadyac revised the script each night from midnight to 4:00 A.M., after Carrey completed taping for *In Living Color.*

Shadyac, who doubled as the movie's director, handed free rein to his friend to fashion the character of Ace Ventura. He admits the move was a gamble, since Carrey had never appeared in a leading role, and he realized that it "would either make or destroy our careers. But Jim and I were in agreement that if we were going to light a stink bomb, let's make it a very unique stink bomb."[104]

Carrey fashioned a most unusual character for the movie. He combined elements from Peter Sellers, Robin Williams, and Jerry Lewis to create a detective who has to locate the Miami Dolphins' missing mascot, a dolphin named Snowflake. He brought every aspect of his talent into the film, including zany humor; an opening sequence in which he walks, trots, and dances his way along the street, brilliantly mimicking John Travolta in *Saturday Night Fever*, and impressions of former president Richard Nixon and Scotty, the engineer from *Star Trek*.

"I've always been gangly—spastic is the word, I think," states Carrey. "I've just basically harnessed spasticness."[105] His energetic performance poked fun at the typical leading man who exudes charm and intelligence. Carrey's aim in making the movie was simple: He wanted to make the audience laugh. "I'm not an expert on anything but laughs. I just know how to make people feel good."[106]

Jim Carrey's first leading role was for the movie Ace Ventura: Pet Detective. *Creating his own character for the script, Carrey's humor was unmatched.*

Carrey achieved stardom by simply being himself, by doing what he had done all his life. Director Peter Farrelly, who would later direct him in the movie *Dumb and Dumber*, describes Carrey as a

> very sweet guy—he's got a big heart, a lot of soul—but he's a tortured animal. My metaphor for Jim is a dog who's constantly beaten up by his owner. The dog can't figure out why. He tries everything to please his owner. He walks on his hind legs; he juggles. Nothing works. Then one day the circus comes along and scoops him up, and he makes a career out of it.[107]

While movie critics assailed *Ace Ventura* as juvenile and lacking substance, the public loved Carrey's first major effort. He received a hint of the favorable reaction when he surreptitiously entered a Los Angeles theater and watched the audience, mainly of college age, howl throughout the showing. They loved his wild portrayal and steady stream of jokes. Nothing in the film challenged the viewers' intelligence; they merely had to sit back and enjoy the experience.

"He's brought comedy back to its, yes, dumb roots," stated an article in *Newsweek* magazine in one of the few positive reviews. The writer called Carrey "an explosion of pure energy that's somehow anarchic and innocent, a fusion of vulgarity and grace."[108]

Effects on His Personal Life

As a result of the triumph of *Ace Ventura*, substantial offers poured in. Morgan Creek, the production company that financed the film, had initially hesitated to sign Carrey to a $1 million contract for a sequel. But after analyzing the returns, Morgan Creek handed the comedian close to $7 million for the next installment. Another producer who had been reluctant to pay Carrey $1 million to star in the movie *Dumb and Dumber* also increased the ante to $7 million.

But professional success did not translate to success in Carrey's private life. His marriage to Melissa fell apart. He admits that the strain of filming a major picture and the demands of being a star made him difficult to live with.

Carrey the Songwriter

After completing *Ace Ventura: Pet Detective*, Carrey traveled to Europe with his close friend, songwriter Phil Roy. While in Paris, Roy purchased a huge painting that depicted scenes of heaven and hell and had it shipped to his home in Los Angeles.

When the painting arrived, Carrey held it up against a wall so that Roy could determine where to hang the piece of art. However, as Roy Trakin related in *Jim Carrey Unmasked!*, Roy could not see the top half and asked Carrey to "Move heaven down here."

Carrey thought that phrase would make a great title for a song, and over the next three weeks he and Roy labored over the lyrics. When they had completed the romantic ballad, they sent it to the New Age duo Tuck and Patti, who selected it from a collection of hundreds to include on their newest album.

When Patti Cathcart, one of the singers, first heard the song, she knew it would be one of the choices. "I have to have it," she mentioned at the time. "Then I found out Jim Carrey was responsible for the idea—and who would have thought, after seeing Jim's movies, that he would come up with such sweet, romantic subject matter?"

Carrey and Roy continued their songwriting career and have written six songs together.

Living with me this last couple of years is like living with an astronaut—it's not the most rewarding experience. It's like, I just came back from the moon, don't ask me to take the garbage out. I can relax, but not at the prescribed times, necessarily, and when you're married, you've got to have time for this and that and it's just . . . impossible.[109]

When Carrey came home from work, he wanted to be left alone so he could create more ideas, while Melissa and Jane needed his attention. In addition, he tried to cope with his anxieties about success and his feelings toward his parents. According to Melissa, Carrey required more affection than she could give. "Jim is an extremely depressive person. I know, because I would sit up counseling him through it until 4 or 5 in the morning on many, many nights. At night he has to face himself, and he so much does not want to do that that this adrenalin rushes up in him."[110]

The marital difficulties affected Carrey on the set. When Tom Shadyac found his friend alone in his trailer in tears, they chatted about the situation. Before they returned to start filming, Carrey dripped water into Shadyac's eyes so the crew would think the two had been discussing Shadyac's problems.

When Melissa told him that he either had to tend to his family and help out around the house or the two would have to part, Carrey moved out. He eventually filed for divorce, and after an acrimonious legal battle to determine the amount of child support, Carrey agreed to a generous settlement for his daughter.

Relations are on a more even keel now. "He's a good father," explains Melissa. "Given that his priority is work and everything else comes second, he does pretty good." [111]

Carrey wonders whether he will ever achieve a stable personal relationship because he knows that he puts so much effort

Jim Carrey remained an involved father after his divorce from wife Melissa, and was sure to include his daughter Jane in his handprint ceremony at Hollywood's Mann's Chinese Theater.

into his work. "I can see a real challenge in my life will be to settle myself down enough to be with someone. Maybe it's not
meant to be for me." [112]

The Mask

Carrey stepped immediately from *Ace Ventura* into an even bigger
role as *The Mask*'s Stanley Ipkiss, a meek bank clerk who trans-
forms into a superhero when he puts on an ancient mask. The
movie featured incredible special effects that, added to Carrey's
repertoire of physical stunts, fashioned a memorable experience.

Carrey spent four hours in makeup each day while experts
added the unique mask. To avoid hiding Carrey's ability to con-
tort his face, the mask was designed so that Carrey's facial expressions could be seen through the makeup.

Carrey frequently upstaged the mask. When Carrey visited
George Lucas's Industrial Light and Magic, the company that was
responsible for the most advanced special effects techniques used
in motion pictures, he put on such an amazing display of physical
talent that one technician asked, "What the hell do you need us
for?" [113] The film's director, Charles Russell, estimated that Carrey's
talents probably saved producers $1 million in optical effects.

His role in *The Mask* was so physically demanding that Carrey often left the set with aching muscles, black-and-blue arms
and legs, and cuts and bruises. A writer for *Time* magazine reported in August 1994 that, in the movie, Carrey "can turn the
simple act of listening into power aerobics. His laser stare becomes maniacally penetrating; turning to hear a question, he
nearly gives himself whiplash." [114] At the same time he exhibited
unexpected finesse and grace in a lengthy dance sequence with
actress Cameron Diaz.

The movie premiered in July 1994 and exceeded the records
set by *Ace Ventura*. More than $25 million poured in on its open-
ing weekend, and the movie eventually earned $120 million in
the United States and over $300 million worldwide. In a few
months Carrey had registered two blockbuster movies.

Although reviews of the movie were mixed, Carrey received
acclaim. *Time* magazine wrote that Carrey "is his own best special
effect, the first star who *is* a live-action toon." [115] *Rolling Stone*

magazine called the movie the funniest of the summer and mentioned of Carrey, "Call him jerkier than Jerry Lewis, geekier
than Jim Varney, and more manic than Robin Williams. . . . Carrey is a comic fireball in a tour de force display of physical antics that should convert his most rabid detractors." The reviewer
added that Carrey proved he could handle tender scenes as well
as the physically crazy episodes. "Those who believe that nothing short of Prozac can slow Carrey down will welcome his
sweetness with Diaz as Stanley tries to express his feelings for
Tina without relying on the mask." [116]

Playing Stanley Ipkiss was almost like playing himself. Just as
Ipkiss wants people to accept him for who he is and not because he

The movie The
Mask *provided
Carrey with his
second leading role
and proved to be a
great success.*

The humorous antics and surprising acting talent Carrey displayed in The Mask *solidified his popularity.*

is a superhero, so Carrey hopes that the public will judge him on his merits and faults as an individual, not on his status as a movie star. He also relates to Ipkiss's desire to accomplish something special, to be the average man who performs above-average deeds.

With money pouring in, for the first time in his life Carrey could stop worrying about finances. In 1994, he purchased a 1965 robin's egg–blue Thunderbird and a $4 million mansion in the exclusive Brentwood section of Los Angeles, complete with two master suites, chauffeur's quarters, a tennis court, a swimming pool, a lagoon, and a waterfall.

Father's Death

Success was bittersweet, though, since his parents did not live to see most of it. His mother had died before *Ace Ventura*, and while Percy Carrey lived long enough to share his son's early fame, he died from cancer in 1994, shortly after *Ace Ventura* and *The Mask* hit theaters. At his funeral, an emotional Carrey took the post-dated check for $10 million out of his wallet and placed it in his father's coffin. Since he had now reached his dream and had begun to earn millions for his work, Carrey believed the check belonged with his father, who had abandoned his dreams years before. The check "was a connection between us," says Carrey. "It was an important dream for him, too." [117]

Dumb and Dumber

In his next film, *Dumb and Dumber*, Carrey played the inept Lloyd Christmas. Christmas and his equally bumbling friend Harry Dunne, played by Jeff Daniels, travel the nation bouncing from one crisis to another as they attempt to return a lost suitcase. "The movie is about two of the dumbest guys in the history of the world going on a road trip," explains Daniels, "who do some of the dumbest things known to man . . . and live to tell about it." [118]

To create Lloyd Christmas, Carrey removed the crown from a chipped front tooth and added a touch of Spock from *Star Trek* and a touch of Jerry Lewis in *The Nutty Professor*. He hoped to deliver a totally bizarre leading character who was unlike his previous roles.

Carrey received $7 million for the movie. He explained that when some actors begin making large amounts of money, they shrink from accepting new challenges. He did not want to fall into that trap. Instead, he decided "this is where I take that leading man thing they're expecting and turn it inside out. So I had this character with a chipped tooth like he smashed himself in the face with a ball-peen hammer and they loved it." [119] Again, Carrey took a risk to further his career.

Jim Carrey continued to achieve success and develop as an actor with his performance in Dumb and Dumber.

Jimmy Stewart

Though Carrey admired many entertainers and adapted their character-istics, one man stood above the rest: famed actor Jimmy Stewart. Known for playing roles in which the average man conquers overwhelming odds, Stewart earned a spot in fans' hearts with movies such as *Mr. Smith Goes to Washington* and *It's a Wonderful Life*. As a youth Carrey watched Stew-art's movies whenever they played on television, and he was determined that one day he would star in a movie that would be favorably compared to Stewart's.

In the late 1980s, shortly be-fore Carrey joined the cast of *In Living Color*, he met his idol. One Christmas season Carrey learned that Stewart had agreed to give a reading from the Bible while an or-chestra played holiday mu-sic. He attended, and after the performance, he walked up and introduced himself to Stewart.

Carrey is a big fan of well-known actor Jimmy Stewart.

As he related in December 1995 to Martha Sherrill, a writer for *Esquire* magazine, "This was like a rock concert for me. I mean, it was Jimmy Stewart, and I would have camped out all night. And inside, I just sat there with my mouth gaping open in the front pew, like it was Pearl Jam or something."

When he shook hands with Jimmy Stewart, Carrey lost all composure and started to imitate the actor. Stewart did not know what to make of this unusual introduction. As Carrey said, "I was just goo-goo over him, and he got embarrassed and got red and walked away."

Once filming began, no one knew what Carrey might do. The director learned to keep a camera on the star even when an-other actor had the lines or after he yelled "Cut!" in case Carrey spun off into an improvisational gem.

Daniels played right along. Though executives wanted a younger actor to play Harry Dunne, Carrey had asked for Jeff Daniels because he hoped to learn from an actor who had won acclaim for his work in such dramatic films as *Gettysburg* and *Terms of Endearment.* Carrey states that Daniels "is a quality actor, and at this point I want to work with people who can challenge me to be better." [120]

The pair formed an instant rapport that translated to the film. Each day the two actors prepared to be "dumb" in different ways. According to Carrey, "When the cameras roll, we just get the glassy, 'I-just-ate-lead-paint-for-breakfast' look. We don't gear up for it. We gear down." Daniels explains that "You basically empty your head. You go blank. You try to get the I.Q. down as close to zero as possible and still make the characters believable. If people see this movie and can think of anyone who is dumber than we are, then we haven't done our job." [121]

The actors devolved into two little kids who tried to top each other. Many days they walked onto the set, asked the director if there was any room to expand the scene, then took off. Daniels recalls that Carrey, "who only needs a little crack in the door,

Jim Carrey and Jeff Daniels developed a close bond while working together on their film Dumb and Dumber.

would be ready with a whole bunch of ideas. So ten minutes before we shot, we'd make changes that worked really well, and we went with them." [122]

Director Peter Farrelly knew he was capturing on film a special chemistry between Carrey and Daniels, who obviously enjoyed working with each other. What impressed him even more, though, was Carrey's ability to convey tenderness and vulnerability. Lloyd Christmas falls in love with the character played by actress Lauren Holly, and Carrey convincingly presented the joy and anguish of early love. In another scene in the movie Lloyd stares out a window and sighs dejectedly about his abysmal life, "I don't want to be a nobody all my life. I want to be somebody." [123] Farrelly directed seven different takes of that scene, which required Carrey to cry on cue, and each time tears filled Carrey's eyes at the correct moment. "His emotions are at his fingertips," [124] says Farrelly.

Critics and Fans Disagree

The movie opened on December 16, 1994, and received the familiar reaction: Many critics hated the film, but fans swarmed to purchase tickets. Critics complained that the film relied too much on bathroom humor—jokes about bodily functions and passing gas—and that it required little intelligence to understand its gags.

A writer for *Rolling Stone* magazine concluded that "The [advertising] poster is funnier than anything in the movie," and the *L.A. Weekly* wrote that the movie was "flatly directed, sloppily edited and altogether inept." However, the same reviewer added, "And, oh yeah, I laughed my ass off. . . . The movie is essentially a chance to let Carrey rip, which he does over and over and over and over again." [125]

When the movie topped the $100 million mark, Carrey boasted three straight box-office smashes in one year, a feat that few Hollywood personalities could match. His 1994 trio grossed $550 million and established Jim Carrey as a star. He was nominated for, but did not receive, a Golden Globe as Best Actor in a Comedy or Musical, and he received the National Association of Theater Owners' Comedy Star of the Year Award. In his acceptance, he told the theater owners that if it were not for his

Although critics panned Dumb and Dumber *in reviews, audiences loved it—the movie grossed over $100 million at the box office.*

movies, "I'd have no creative outlet and would surely have to be institutionalized."[126]

Carrey claimed that he was happy his success had not come quickly because he would feel as though he had not deserved it. By working the comedy club route, by enduring the numbing auditions, and by acting in bit parts and television shows, he had earned the right to success. When he dwelt on 1994, Carrey said, "It's like Cinderella. Except it's never going to be midnight. . . . Isn't it incredible? There are times when you say, 'What the hell is going on?'"[127]

Just at the moment when he should have thoroughly enjoyed the many blessings that had come his way, Carrey unsheathed the skeptical side born of desperate times growing up in Canada. Though he appeared to be financially set for life and his career was on a fast track, Carrey said, "As it is, I still every once in a while think, 'Ooh, what if they take it away?'"[128]

In Love Again

While filming *Dumb and Dumber* Carrey fell in love with his leading lady, Lauren Holly. Holly relates that Carrey walked up to her one day and said, "I would like to be your girlfriend. Would you be my girlfriend?" Holly adds, "What girl on the planet could refuse when someone says that?"[129]

People on the set first noticed something had developed when the director's chairs used by the costars inched closer together. Carrey had failed in his first attempt at a stable relationship and wondered whether love was "possible forever and ever." He stated that he hoped it could be and declared that "I am absolutely head over heels in love right now. It's wonderful."[130]

Holly fell for him, too, even though she compared the unpredictable Carrey to a "runaway train."[131] Joel Schumacher, who would direct Carrey in later films, says that Carrey "looks like the guy every mother wants their daughter to marry." However,

Carrey fell in love with and became engaged to actress Lauren Holly after they worked together on Dumb and Dumber. *They were married in September 1996.*

Schumacher adds, the unpredictable comedian usually "acts like the guy they usually *do* marry."[132]

After driving up the Pacific Coast Highway to locate a suitable oceanside setting, Carrey and Holly married in September 1996. They then jetted off for a honeymoon on a Caribbean island.

Even with the company of a new bride, Carrey would not believe that happiness was secure. He contends that it is more sensible to remain cautious and hope for the best.

> I hate it when I see people go on talk shows, and they just married the supermodel of the century, and they are like, "This is it, absolutely." That to me is arrogant in the face of nature. It'd be an incredibly wonderful thing if I end up being, like, eighty years old, and me and Lauren are heading out having a great old time. But as soon as you say you *know*, the universe will prove you wrong.[133]

Carrey refuses to trust happiness because, in his experience, it has arrived and departed in rapid shifts.

As with his relationship with Melissa, Carrey again needed space to wind down from the pressures of entertaining. He expected that Holly would understand his urge to be alone. "I love Lauren and my daughter [Jane] and I need a home base. I just need to know I can say, 'I'm going to the Arctic,' and have Lauren go, 'Great! See you later. I know you need to do this.'"[134] This attitude contributed to problems in their marriage, and after ten tumultuous months the two divorced. However, in 1998 the couple reunited.

Besides his quest for personal happiness, Carrey searched for ways to expand into dramatic roles. His work in the mid-1990s would provide that expansion.

Chapter 6

"How Dare He Try to Do Something Different"

CARREY'S GOOD FORTUNE continued into 1995. In February, two television networks announced that they were producing Saturday morning cartoon shows based on each of Carrey's three 1994 films. Carrey continued his streak of hit movies with two more comedic roles. However, to avoid being typecast as only a comedian, Carrey pursued serious parts as well. He found the transition bumpier than expected.

Batman Forever

Carrey's next role, villain Edward Nygma in the *Batman* sequel, *Batman Forever,* seemed tailor-made for him since it combined outrageous actions with humor. Robin Williams appeared to be the leading candidate to play Nygma, but when he turned down the role, Carrey was signed.

Other actors from the movie quickly learned that they were in for an unusual experience working beside Carrey. Val Kilmer, who landed the role of Batman, had never seen Carrey perform before. He explains that when he found out the comedian had been signed, "I got *Ace Ventura,* and all I had to do was watch the opening deliveryman sequence. I called up the studio and said [sarcastically], 'Well, this'll be fun.'" [135]

A problem quickly developed on the set. Kilmer and another costar, Tommy Lee Jones, complained that Carrey's over-the-top antics attempted to upstage them. Kilmer and Jones worried that Carrey would capture most of the public's attention once the movie hit theaters.

Tommy Lee Jones, who carried an impressive list of theatrical accomplishments into the movie, eventually expressed admiration for Carrey's acting. Director Joel Schumacher claims that "Tommy is used to stealing the show. He definitely met his match here and many times was surprised by it. It kept everybody on their toes. Jim is such an athlete, and athletes know their personal best."[136]

Schumacher respected Carrey's dedication to his craft, as well. Each day, Carrey arrived on the set on time and fully prepared, qualities that Schumacher had not seen in other young actors and actresses.

> I went through the era of young stars coming in late, being lazy and stoned, wearing sunglasses and being more into wearing sunglasses than the work. And they aren't stars anymore. This new group of people like Jim Carrey and

Acting alongside Tommy Lee Jones in Batman Forever, *Carrey once again delivered a hit performance as the villain Edward Nygma.*

Sandra Bullock and Brad Pitt and Chris O'Donnell—are really dedicated to being good actors. Fame is really secondary. I've never seen anyone work harder than Jim. And everything that appears spontaneous is the result of hours and hours of preparation.[137]

Batman Forever opened in June 1995 with the biggest opening weekend in Hollywood history—$53.3 million. For the fourth time in a row, Carrey starred in a blockbuster picture that earned more than $100 million at the box office.

Ace Ventura: When Nature Calls

Later that year Carrey starred in *Ace Ventura: When Nature Calls,* the sequel to *Ace Ventura: Pet Detective.* "I'm looking forward to getting back to the character," said Carrey before filming started. "I have such fun doing it."[138]

The experience was not a happy one, however. He and director Tom DeCerchio battled over the film's contents, and supermodel Georgianna Robertson, cast in one of the film's supporting roles, left the production after only one day. Since the film was based on Carrey's role of Ace Ventura, he could not quit, so he remained in his trailer on the set to express his discontent with DeCerchio. Eventually, the director was replaced by Carrey's old friend Steve Oedekerk.

Though the movie was a modest hit, critics lambasted the plot and stated that certain scenes insulted Native Americans. Scenes that depicted tribal rituals in a comic light were described as offensive.

Carrey's stream of jokes seemed to have been tossed into the movie for humor's sake rather than to support the plot, which had Carrey searching for an albino bat. Unlike the first *Ace Ventura,* which displayed a flair for originality, the sequel lacked vitality and depended heavily on bathroom humor. Many fans purchased tickets with the hope of seeing something similar to *Ace Ventura: Pet Detective,* but they left disappointed.

Though the film turned a profit for investors, most fans and critics were disappointed with the comedian's latest effort. Irritated at the outcome, Carrey felt he needed a new direction.

Carrey faced creative restraints in Ace Ventura: When Nature Calls *and was disappointed with the film's lack of success in theaters.*

The Cable Guy

Carrey and his managers had discussed ways to expand Carrey's career, and to that end they searched for the proper vehicle to begin the transition to dramatic roles. Other actors who started in comedy had accomplished the feat. Tom Hanks, who rose to fame in comedies like *Splash* and *Bachelor Party*, easily jumped to drama with *Nothing in Common* and the Oscar-winning performances in *Philadelphia* and 1994's *Forrest Gump*. Comedian Robin Williams had successfully entered the dramatic world with stunning roles in *Dead Poets Society* and *Awakenings*.

Carrey expected that he could follow a similar path. In a move his managers believed would guarantee success, they planned to place their star in a drama, follow that with a comedy, back to another drama, then a comedy, and so on. That way if one of the serious features bombed, Carrey could balance the loss with a box-office hit.

Carrey's initial step was to star in *The Cable Guy*, a movie about a lonely cable installer. The executives handed Carrey a huge $20 million contract and creative control over the movie, but in return they expected him to deliver another hit in the vein of *Ace Ventura: Pet Detective* and *Dumb and Dumber*. Studio head Mark Canton selected *The Cable Guy* to anchor the studio's 1996 summer lineup, and anything less than a box-office triumph, especially in light of Carrey's lucrative salary, would be a financial disaster. One studio executive referred to Carrey's contract for the film, which made him Hollywood's highest-paid actor, and said, "Jim may be the biggest star in the world, and we're going to find out." [139]

Carrey made plans to make a black comedy, a movie that contains some humor but stresses a serious point—in this case that modern society so depends on electronic media, especially television, that personal relationships and responsibilities toward one another are shoved aside. He turned the cable installer into a somber loner who, ignored by his mother, spends his maturing

"Keep Me Human"

Jim Carrey understands that, with the fame he has achieved, his life will never be what it had been before. However, he tries to avoid falling into the trap of thinking he is more important than others. He mentioned in a 1996 interview with newspaper reporter Bob Strauss that when he finishes shooting a scene, he likes to relax.

> I've always found people who have to be "on" all the time sad. I know a lot of comedians, and I know the ones who can actually sit in a room and have a human conversation and the ones that are just waiting for their moment to chime in with something funny. They want to be part of it, but they're really not interested in anything anybody has to say.

While adulation swirls about his life and reporters follow every move he makes, Carrey clutches onto one hope—that he does not lose perspective. "Obviously this is an ordeal. At the same time, it's an amazing and wonderful period in my life. It is something I have to learn: how to pick up this mantle and be a human being. I have disclaimers in every prayer: 'Keep me human. Let me like myself.'"

years before a television set. Now an adult, the cable installer desperately seeks friendship. Much of the movie focuses on his attempt to befriend the character played by actor Matthew Broderick; when Broderick shuns him, the cable installer plans his vengeance.

The movie meant so much to Carrey that he demanded perfection in each scene. Broderick explains that Carrey "will not rest until a scene is perfect. Sometimes that means doing a lot of takes."[140] Carrey felt pressure to produce a hit, and frequent visits to the set from studio executives emphasized the point. Director Ben Stiller says of the manner in which Carrey handled the stress, "I was very impressed with the way he dealt with it. It didn't inhibit him. He never really got concerned that he was going to be cutting off part of his audience or alienating people."[141]

To their dismay, executives watched helplessly as Carrey transformed the initial idea of a light comedy into a satiric commentary on parenting and the influence of television on society. Since they had given Carrey creative control over the film, executives had to rely on Carrey's judgment.

Though the film grossed $20 million its first weekend, Carrey's fans walked away disappointed. Receipts plummeted the second week, indicating that negative word of mouth would doom the film. An Internet poll of Carrey fans revealed that 73 percent disliked *The Cable Guy*, and fans under age twenty—the core of Carrey's audience—stayed away in droves. Critics joined fans by ridiculing the film as an unpleasant story that depressed the audience. One reviewer compared Carrey's message to "a person with a disease coughing in a crowded room."[142]

"I had parents come up to me and say that their kid was crying when they left," says Carrey. "I thought, I don't want your kid to be upset, but you know what? It's not going to hurt him to be upset. The trouble is this . . . mentality that life has to be completely happy all the time."[143]

Carrey claimed that the studio doomed the movie by advertising it as a comedy rather than what it was. He contended that the heavy criticism did not erupt because of any poor work he did but because he turned out something unexpected. A bitter Carrey asserts that "It wasn't 'Jim Carrey's work is not good.' It was 'How dare he try to do something different?' It was an industry ambush."[144]

While he hoped audiences would watch the movie with a willingness to explore deeper themes, he did not believe he had created a depressing film. "I don't think *Cable Guy* is that disturbing. It's a bit of a shift, but there's still a wild character there for people to grab onto. I just think there are more levels, there's more going on." [145]

Although The Cable Guy *was a box-office flop, Carrey's performance proved that he could develop a multidimensional character, not just a humorous one.*

Most observers disagree with Carrey's assessment. Instead of acting in a serious movie with a pleasant edge, he produced a nasty film that irritated fans. Robin Williams and Tom Hanks starred in likable dramatic films and moved on to bigger success. Jim Carrey still had to find the way.

Liar, Liar

After the failures of *The Cable Guy* and *Ace Ventura: When Nature Calls,* Carrey needed a hit to restore his image. Universal Studios provided him with such a film. In *Liar, Liar,* Carrey plays Fletcher Reede, an attorney who regularly disappoints his five-year-old son, Max, by promising visits and then showing up late or forgetting them entirely. Divorced from his wife, Reede devotes full attention to his occupation and realizes how much he loves his son only when he learns Max might move east with his mother.

When Reede fails to appear at his son's birthday party, Max, again disappointed that his father had not kept his word, blows out the candles on his birthday cake and wishes that his father would be unable to tell a lie for twenty-four hours. From then on, Carrey strings together a series of hilarious encounters in which he disturbs coworkers and passersby with his painfully honest responses. Gradually, Reede realizes how frequently he lies and how much of a disappointment he has been to his son.

Carrey excels at more than just comedy in this movie. After his ex-wife informs Reede that she is moving away, a somber Reede tries to figure out a way to keep his son close to him. Through a string of events, alternatingly funny and touching, he succeeds in reuniting with both Max and his ex-wife.

Carrey took another risk with this character in that Reede, while comical, presents a serious side to the audience. Carrey could have safely fallen back on his Lloyd Christmas–type persona and guaranteed another hit, but instead he delivered a complex individual who laughs on the outside to cover the pain hidden inside. Bobby Farrelly, who cowrote the script for *Dumb and Dumber*, explains that "Jim can't do the same character over and over. That's what producers would love him to do—until people can't stand the sight of him." [146]

With his Golden Globe–nominated performance in the movie Liar, Liar *Carrey proved successful in more serious roles.*

Carrey triumphed in this movie because, unlike the character in *The Cable Guy*, Fletcher Reede presents a likable side. Reede typified numerous individuals who experience similar crises, so people in the audience could relate to the pain that both Max and Fletcher endured. Carrey did not have to search for a way to reflect the agony since he had lived the situation all his life, first as a child staring at disappointment, then as an adult enduring the guilt of separation from his daughter. "If you're from a broken marriage and you had children," says Carrey, "no matter how diligent you are about seeing your kid, you still have these feelings that it's not enough."[147]

Carrey loved the role because it examined the importance of the family unit.

> *Liar, Liar* was just such a wonderful concept because it's an opportunity for me to actually have a [family] relationship. But at the same time, it has that kind of frustrating, John Cleese kind of situation to it, where you have the opportunity to go completely mad.[148]

Liar, Liar restored Carrey to box-office success. The film grossed close to $200 million, and Carrey received a Golden Globe Best Actor nomination. Though the movie offered him the opportunity to deliver a many-layered interpretation of Fletcher Reede, Carrey still sought the straight dramatic role in which he could showcase his skill as an actor. The movie arrived with 1998's *The Truman Show.*

Chapter 7

"Fame Is What He Wanted, You Know"

M ANY HOLLYWOOD OBSERVERS predicted that *The Truman Show* would flop like *The Cable Guy*, but Carrey determinedly pushed forward. He had taken risks throughout his career, and *The Truman Show* was simply one more step along that hazardous path.

Carrey Jumps at *The Truman Show*

Taking the lead role in *The Truman Show* posed few concerns for Carrey. He states that

> I don't want to stay in the same gear all the time. You see it . . . in people who are so afraid of losing their status that they don't do anything different. I'd rather lose it all and not do the same thing every time than pander to this imaginary thing that's my strength.[149]

Carrey freely accepted risks because he believed that only by taking risks does one gain the largest triumphs.

In *The Truman Show* Carrey portrayed thirty-year-old Truman Burbank, an insurance agent whose entire life has been turned into a television soap opera. Without Truman's knowledge, five thousand cameras have recorded every event in his life in Seahaven, Florida, a Disney-like community created for this popular television show; live footage was beamed into households all over the world.

Two factors made Carrey more optimistic about this movie's chances for success. First, the movie's director, Peter Weir, had successfully handled Harrison Ford's transition from *Star Wars* to dramatic roles with *Witness* and Robin Williams's foray away from comedy with *Dead Poets Society*. Second, Carrey planned to avoid the mistake producers made in advertising *The Cable Guy* as a comedy. Publicity would inform moviegoers that the film contained serious dramatic overtones.

Carrey understood Truman Burbank because in many ways the two personalities were similar. Carrey had spent most of his early life trying to ensure the happiness of his parents and siblings, and in Truman Burbank he saw "a guy who, for some reason, deep down, has this melancholy. He's a wonderful human being. He wants everybody to be happy, and no one to be burdened by his sadness." [150]

This character, though, tossed an additional challenge to Carrey. Since he would not be hiding under a mask or behind the guise of a wacky character, audiences would tend to see Carrey and Truman Burbank as one and the same. Claims Carrey,

> Truman is a lot more naked than most of the things I've done. When you do a character that's kind of close to yourself, and you strip away the defense mechanisms and the little tricks, . . . that's the scary part. Because then you're giving them a glimpse at yourself. If they reject that, it becomes, "We don't like your essence—you, at the core, we don't like." [151]

One of Carrey's managers, Jimmy Miller, explains that this movie ideally fit into Carrey's plans. "To jump into a heavy war picture or a crime picture would have been crazy. It had to be something like *Truman* that blended comedy and fantasy into something with dramatic underpinnings. I think we all knew *Truman* was the perfect script." [152]

Worried Exhibitors

While Carrey's camp eagerly awaited the public's reaction to *The Truman Show*, most Hollywood producers and nearly every theater owner expected a poor showing. *The Cable Guy*, after all, had bombed, and here was Carrey heading down the dramatic

Many people were skeptical that Carrey could succeed in the dramatic role of Truman Burbank in the movie The Truman Show.

road again. One nervous exhibitor said before the film arrived in his theater chain that "after a huge hit like *Liar, Liar* what do you think exhibitors want from him? They want what the public wants—what works. Of course, everyone's a bit antsy." [153] Carrey gambled that the public would accept quality material no matter who delivered it, and if *The Truman Show* exuded warmth and creativity, the public would embrace it. Besides, Carrey had already delivered a fine dramatic portrayal in *Doing Time on Maple Drive.* He was confident he could do so again.

One reporter for the *Los Angeles Times* analyzed producers' hesitancy in accepting a dramatic Jim Carrey and concluded that the notion that "these exhibitors whine and fret at the expense of the creative life of a man whose films have already made their theaters so much money is outright offensive. What a gang of spoiled brats." [154] The writer added that if the owners had their way, current superstars like Tom Hanks, Robin Williams, and John Travolta would still be stuck in the comedic roles with which they started their careers rather than having branched out into the dramatic field.

The film struck a chord with the public. Peter Weir attended an advance screening to check audience reaction, and one film-goer mentioned to him that "he came out of my film with a very strange feeling. And then, he said, he realized what it was. He was thinking." [155]

Time magazine heralded the film. "You will laugh. You will cry. You will be provoked to ask yourself *why* you feel this way. And for once in a blue moon of movies, you will think." [156]

Critics favorably compared Carrey's performance to that of Tom Hanks in his Oscar-winning film *Forrest Gump*. Talk of an Oscar nomination for Carrey bounced about Hollywood, and exhibitors, delighted that the blockbuster film grossed more than $100 million, grudgingly admitted that the comedian need no longer worry about doubts about his serious acting ability.

Fans Galore

As Carrey's popularity increased, he experienced the positives and negatives of having an adoring public. Invitations pour in—for each one he accepts he declines another twenty—and each

Audiences thoroughly embraced The Truman Show—*it grossed over $100 million at the box office.*

day brings in a flood of new scripts. "It's insane," he explains, "it really is. People come over to my house and say, 'Hey, I have this friend who has a script you should read' and I just take them over to the cupboard and there's literally fifty scripts in there that I need to attend to at some point."[157]

Wherever he goes, fans want to speak with him, touch him, or get his autograph. Women lust after him. He and Lauren Holly walked into a San Antonio, Texas, bar one night and a young woman asked Holly, "Can I hug your boyfriend?" When Holly replied, "Can I hug yours?"[158] the woman drifted away.

In many ways Carrey has become Truman Burbank. He can rarely escape scrutiny, even on vacations, and he has learned to be guarded in what he says. He even expresses concern that the intense scrutiny might one day lead to absurdities. "Am I going to be combing my beard some day, and a little [media] transmitter falls out?"[159]

Although not unexpected, the lack of privacy can be taxing. "The only space I can be private," says Carrey, is on the bus he uses on a set. "Everybody else has the whole of the outdoors to roam around in. I have to fly to Fiji to get that. And I might not get it there. Look at those naked pictures somebody took of Brad Pitt on St. Bart's. It's terrible."[160]

He fears that one of his most effective tools—the ability to quietly observe others—might be voided by all the attention. "I'm afraid, I guess, that I won't be able to watch anymore. Everything I do comes from watching and observing, and I'm concerned that I won't be able to be the watcher because I'm the watched."[161]

Consequently, one pleasure he clutches onto is motorcycle riding. Since he wears a helmet no one recognizes him, and the activity allows him to go anywhere at any time. "It's great," he says. "I can look right at somebody in a car. I'm just normal. Just another carbon-based life-form that nobody needs anything from."[162]

Peter Weir places the situation in proper context. A reporter asked Weir if he thought Jim Carrey was happy, and the director replied,

No. But I don't know whether *I* am. So I could hardly comment on Jim. He's complex, to be able to do what he does. He's certainly fulfilled by the work, so I see him, no doubt, at his happiest. He lives in a fishbowl, and has to be careful of concealed cameras. But Jim can hardly complain. I mean, fame is what he wanted, you know? It's the old fairy tale—be careful of what you wish for.[163]

Recent Projects

Besides *The Truman Show*, Carrey acted in another 1998 film, *Simon Birch*. Though his appearance is limited—he plays an adult character flashing back to his childhood—the movie earned more accolades.

Later that year Carrey completed filming of a new movie titled *Man on the Moon*, the biography of the late comedian Andy Kaufman. Top Hollywood talent sought the role, including Oscar nominee Edward Norton and Oscar winners Kevin Spacey and Nicolas Cage. When Carrey landed the coveted part, he received confirmation that Hollywood finally considered him a serious actor.

Directed by Milos Forman, the movie forced Carrey to analyze his own life. Kaufman, who rose to stardom during the early days of *Saturday Night Live* and in the television series *Taxi*, faced pressures similar to Carrey's. To convey the pain and joy of Andy Kaufman, Carrey had to reexamine his own experiences and emotions.

Carrey, whose films have earned $1.5 billion worldwide at the box office, has also signed to star in *Fool on the Hill*, a movie about a disc jockey who operates a radio station at a mental institution. His broadcast affects the lives of the patients in the institution as well as the residents of the small town in which it is located. He will follow that with remakes of two movies, a comedy called *The Incredible Mr. Limpet*, which will rely heavily on animation, and *The Secret Life of Walter Mitty*, a comedy directed by Ron Howard.

While Carrey earns upwards of $20 million for each film, money does not motivate him. He states that he will always work because "Even if I have $40 million in the bank, if I don't feel that I did a good job that day, I'm a basket case. I'm linked to my work in a probably extremely unhealthy way. It's too important to me." [164]

Carrey's mother used to tell him he was never satisfied with his work, a statement with which Carrey totally agrees. He seeks

Comedian Andy Kaufman (far left) rose to stardom after his role in the television series Taxi. *Carrey's role in the biographical movie of Kaufman,* Man on the Moon, *reminded Carrey of his own life and rise to fame.*

success, which in Carrey's case means perfection. "What success means is being at the top of my game. That's what I want. What I'm still looking for." [165]

Acting is at the core of Carrey's being. When asked what he would have done had he not gone into acting, Carrey readily replies, "I would have become a street person." He adds, "I don't have a trade. There was no choice for me. It makes you work a little harder when you don't have an exit." [166]

Plans for the Future

Though he has long known what he wanted to do with his life, Carrey does not limit where he can go in his chosen field. He believes he is able to do comedy, drama, and a mix of the two. Those who know Carrey best also see him as an incredibly versatile performer. Joel Schumacher is one of those who believes Carrey can succeed in any format.

> Jim is like one of those huge organs in an old church with thousands of pedals and pipes. He can play Jimmy Stewart in *It's A Wonderful Life* or he can play the devil or he can play *Dumb and Dumber*, Laurel and Hardy, or the Marx Brothers. [167]

Carrey asserts the one thing that would destroy his career is complacency. He never wants to be accused of doing the same thing over and over. Though his energetic brand of physical humor has been compared to the style of comedy made famous by Jerry Lewis, Lewis's career serves as a warning to Carrey. "I saw him doing stand-up comedy recently," explains Carrey, "and he's still doing that same squeaky little-boy voice. And the man's sixty years old! Man, it's time to move on." Carrey adds, "I won't be Ace when I'm fifty, but there'll always be moments of craziness. The best characters to me were guys played by Jimmy Stewart: sweet and lovable and fallible. When they got downhearted, people cared about them more. I think Jimmy's a good role model." [168]

Carrey realizes that some fans will continue to demand Ace Ventura, no matter how many dramatic roles he accepts. Some simply do not want him to change. "In this day and age, it'd be,

Carrey Wins Golden Globe

Jim Carrey proved to nervous exhibitors and movie producers that he could successfully cross over from comedy to drama by capturing the 1999 Golden Globe Award for Best Actor in a Drama for his role as Truman Burbank in the film, *The Truman Show*. Dire forecasts by some in the industry warned that a comedian like Carrey could not pull off a dramatic role or make a profit for the studio releasing the film. Carrey quickly silenced the critics on the latter charge when *The Truman Show* soared to the top of the box office.

His touching portrayal of Truman Burbank impressed not only moviegoers, but the Hollywood Foreign Press Association. On January 24, 1999, the group handed Carrey its Golden Globe, considered by many to be a precursor to an Oscar.

Carrey was delighted that others agreed with his contention that he could admirably perform in serious roles, and he hopes that the Golden Globe will quiet those who insist that his is only a comedian.

you know, Van Gogh doing a movie, and they're going, 'Why didn't he lop his other ear off? Sew it back on and lop it off again! We *love* that!'"[169]

Carrey also hopes to eventually erase those lingering doubts that some critics have about his talent. He still feels the barbs reproaching him for his bathroom jokes and juvenile tastes or for the notion that anyone can perform slapstick comedy. Those who appreciate his talent see him as the traditional jester; Carrey's brand of humor makes people laugh and think. But seriousness lingers beneath much of Carrey's humor, and his more recent roles stretch that seriousness to the dramatic arena. As *Newsday* writer Gene Seymour comments, "Carrey's many things, but he's neither simple nor mediocre."[170]

Whatever outcome occurs, Carrey will be onstage, whether it is a movie soundstage or a comedy club platform, for he is the consummate showman. "I've already had so much success, I could quit now and say, 'Thanks very much, you guys have been more than nice to me.' But I really would like to keep working and, hopefully, growing and challenging myself. With luck, the audience will grow along with me, or else I'll lose a few and gain a few in a new area."[171]

Entertaining has always been in his blood, from his earliest days in Canada until more recent times. Carrey can imagine doing nothing else. Even should his movie career crumble or his health deteriorate, Carrey would still try to get a laugh or make an audience think.

> I've always imagined that even if something should happen to me, and—heaven forbid—all I could move was my baby finger, a few months later people would be saying, "Hey, you gotta go down to the club to see what Carrey is doing with his finger, man. It's weird!" [172]

Notes

Introduction: "You're a Big Star Now"

1. Quoted in Scott and Barbara Siegel, eds., *The Jim Carrey Scrapbook*. New York: Citadel Press, 1995, p. 59.
2. Quoted in Siegel, *The Jim Carrey Scrapbook*, p. 73.
3. Quoted in Roy Trakin, *Jim Carrey Unmasked!* New York: St. Martin's, 1995, p. 135.
4. Jeff Strickler, "Call of the Wildman," *Star Tribune*, November 10, 1995, p. 1.
5. Quoted in Judith Graham, ed., *Current Biography Yearbook, 1996*. New York: H. W. Wilson, 1996, p. 77.
6. Quoted in Trakin, *Jim Carrey Unmasked!*, p. 196.
7. Bruce Handy, "Don't Laugh," *Time*, June 1, 1998, pp. 80–81.

Chapter 1: "What Is It About Me That's Going to Be . . . Special?"

8. Quoted in Martha Sherrill, "Renaissance Man," *Esquire*, December 1995, p. 103.
9. Quoted in Siegel, *The Jim Carrey Scrapbook*, p. 31.
10. Quoted in Laurie Lanzen Harris, ed., *Biography Today*. Detroit: Omnigraphics, 1998, p. 36.
11. Quoted in Trakin, *Jim Carrey Unmasked!*, p. 17.
12. Quoted in Siegel, *The Jim Carrey Scrapbook*, p. 34.
13. Quoted in Sherrill, "Renaissance Man," p. 103.
14. Quoted in Trakin, *Jim Carrey Unmasked!*, p. 14.
15. Quoted in Fred Schruers, "Oh, Please Don't Do That," *Rolling Stone*, July 13–27, 1995, p. 73.
16. Quoted in Harris, *Biography Today*, p. 36.
17. Quoted in Harris, *Biography Today*, p. 36.

18. Quoted in Chris Smith, "Do Not Adjust Your Set," *New York*, June 1, 1998, p. 27.
19. Quoted in Schruers, "Oh, Please Don't Do That," p. 73.
20. Quoted in Trakin, *Jim Carrey Unmasked!*, p. 16.
21. Quoted in Trakin, *Jim Carrey Unmasked!*, p. 16.
22. Quoted in Trakin, *Jim Carrey Unmasked!*, pp. 14–15.
23. Quoted in Trakin, *Jim Carrey Unmasked!*, p. 18.
24. Quoted in Harris, *Biography Today*, p. 36.
25. Quoted in Harris, *Biography Today*, p. 36.
26. Quoted in Louise Mooney Collins and Geri J. Speace, eds., *Newsmakers: The People Behind Today's Headlines*. Detroit: Gale Research, 1995, p. 74.

Chapter 2: "Jim Carrey—Here He Comes"

27. Quoted in Bridget Byrne, "*In Living Color*'s Funny Face Plays It Straight," *TV Guide*, March 14, 1992, p. 15.
28. Quoted in Schruers, "Oh, Please Don't Do That," p. 73.
29. Quoted in Jeff Giles, "Funny Face," *Newsweek*, June 26, 1995, p. 51.
30. Quoted in Trakin, *Jim Carrey Unmasked!*, p. 20.
31. Quoted in Kendall Hamilton, "Not Another Pretty Face," *Newsweek*, July 25, 1994, p. 51.
32. Quoted in Karen S. Schneider, "Doing Just Dandy: Fame Offers Jim Carrey the First Dance—and the Last Laugh," *People*, June 24, 1996, p. 2.
33. Quoted in Hamilton, "Not Another Pretty Face," p. 51.
34. Quoted in Schruers, "Oh, Please Don't Do That," p. 73.
35. Quoted in Schruers, "Oh, Please Don't Do That," p. 73.
36. Quoted in Harris, *Biography Today*, pp. 36–37.
37. Quoted in Graham, *Current Biography Yearbook, 1996*, p. 75.
38. Quoted in Giles, "Funny Face," p. 51.
39. Quoted in Giles, "Funny Face," p. 51.
40. Quoted in Harris, *Biography Today*, p. 37.
41. Quoted in Graham, *Current Biography Yearbook, 1996*, p. 75.
42. Quoted in Trakin, *Jim Carrey Unmasked!*, p. 22.
43. Quoted in Graham, *Current Biography Yearbook, 1996*, p. 75.
44. Quoted in Collins and Speace, *Newsmakers*, p. 36.
45. Quoted in Siegel, *The Jim Carrey Scrapbook*, p. 74.

46. Quoted in Trakin, *Jim Carrey Unmasked!*, p. 23.

47. Quoted in Siegel, *The Jim Carrey Scrapbook*, p. 36.

48. Quoted in "Jim Carrey: The Joker's Wild," *A & E's Biography*.

49. Quoted in Collins and Speace, *Newsmakers*, p. 74.

50. Quoted in "Jim Carrey: The Joker's Wild," *A & E's Biography*.

51. Quoted in Siegel, *The Jim Carrey Scrapbook*, pp. 33–34.

52. Quoted in Siegel, *The Jim Carrey Scrapbook*, p. 37.

53. Quoted in Harris, *Biography Today*, p. 38.

Chapter 3: "Sometimes You Have to Cry Before You Laugh"

54. Quoted in Siegel, *The Jim Carrey Scrapbook*, p. 37.

55. Quoted in Trakin, *Jim Carrey Unmasked!*, p. 31.

56. Quoted in Trakin, *Jim Carrey Unmasked!*, p. 35.

57. Quoted in Schruers, "Oh, Please Don't Do That," p. 74.

58. Quoted in Trakin, *Jim Carrey Unmasked!*, p. 36.

59. Quoted in Trakin, *Jim Carrey Unmasked!*, p. 40.

60. Quoted in Byrne, "*In Living Color*'s Funny Face Plays It Straight," p. 14.

61. Quoted in Harris, *Biography Today*, p. 39.

62. Quoted in Harris, *Biography Today*, p. 39.

63. Quoted in Graham, *Current Biography Yearbook, 1996*, p. 76.

64. Quoted in Harris, *Biography Today*, p. 44.

65. Quoted in Giles, "Funny Face," p. 53.

66. Quoted in Siegel, *The Jim Carrey Scrapbook*, p. 31.

67. Quoted in Bob Strauss, "Carrey on the Line," *Star Tribune*, June 14, 1996, p. 3.

68. Quoted in Trakin, *Jim Carrey Unmasked!*, p. 41.

69. Quoted in Strauss, "Carrey on the Line," p. 2.

70. Quoted in Trakin, *Jim Carrey Unmasked!*, p. 43.

71. Quoted in Harris, *Biography Today*, p. 44.

72. Quoted in Harris, *Biography Today*, p. 40.

73. Quoted in Siegel, *The Jim Carrey Scrapbook*, p. 120.

74. Quoted in Schruers, "Oh, Please Don't Do That," p. 74.

75. Quoted in Harris, *Biography Today*, p. 40.

76. Quoted in Collins and Speace, *Newsmakers*, p. 75.

77. Quoted in Harris, *Biography Today*, p. 40.

78. Quoted in Trakin, *Jim Carrey Unmasked!*, p. 60.

79. Quoted in Trakin, *Jim Carrey Unmasked!*, p. 39.

Chapter 4: "I Always Kind of Believed in Miracles"

80. Quoted in Trakin, *Jim Carrey Unmasked!*, p. 53.

81. Quoted in Siegel, *The Jim Carrey Scrapbook*, p. 47.

82. Quoted in Hamilton, "Not Another Pretty Face," p. 50.

83. Quoted in Sherrill, "Renaissance Man," p. 104.

84. Quoted in "Jim Carrey: The Joker's Wild," *A & E's Biography*.

85. Quoted in Giles, "Funny Face," p. 52.

86. Quoted in Giles, "Funny Face," p. 52.

87. Quoted in Harris, *Biography Today*, p. 39.

88. Quoted in Schruers, "Oh, Please Don't Do That," p. 73.

89. Quoted in Sherrill, "Renaissance Man," p. 103.

90. Quoted in Trakin, *Jim Carrey Unmasked!*, pp. 75–76.

91. Quoted in Siegel, *The Jim Carrey Scrapbook*, p. 52.

92. Quoted in Siegel, *The Jim Carrey Scrapbook*, p. 27.

93. Quoted in Giles, "Funny Face," p. 52.

94. Quoted in Siegel, *The Jim Carrey Scrapbook*, p. 53.

95. Quoted in Trakin, *Jim Carrey Unmasked!*, p. 83.

96. Quoted in Trakin, *Jim Carrey Unmasked!*, p. 84.

97. Quoted in Byrne, "*In Living Color*'s Funny Face Plays It Straight," p. 15.

98. Quoted in Byrne, "*In Living Color*'s Funny Face Plays It Straight," p. 15.

99. Quoted in Trakin, *Jim Carrey Unmasked!*, p. 93.

100. Quoted in Trakin, *Jim Carrey Unmasked!*, p. 94.

101. Quoted in Byrne, "*In Living Color*'s Funny Face Plays It Straight," p. 14.

102. Quoted in Trakin, *Jim Carrey Unmasked!*, p. 165.

Chapter 5: "I've . . . Harnessed Spasticness"

103. Quoted in Trakin, *Jim Carrey Unmasked!*, p. 101.

104. Quoted in Harris, *Biography Today*, p. 41.

105. Quoted in Siegel, *The Jim Carrey Scrapbook*, p. 24.

106. Quoted in Sherrill, "Renaissance Man," p. 106.

107. Quoted in Handy, "Don't Laugh," p. 82.

108. Quoted in Graham, *Current Biography Yearbook, 1996*, pp. 74–75.

109. Quoted in Harris, *Biography Today*, p. 43.

110. Quoted in Schruers, "Oh, Please Don't Do That," p. 125.

111. Quoted in Schneider, "Doing Just Dandy," p. 3.

112. Quoted in Siegel, *The Jim Carrey Scrapbook*, p. 76.

113. Quoted in Trakin, *Jim Carrey Unmasked!*, p. 133.

114. Quoted in Richard Corliss, "Smile! Your Life's on TV," *Time,* June 1, 1998, p. 56.

115. Quoted in Collins and Speace, *Newsmakers*, p. 75.

116. Quoted in Trakin, *Jim Carrey Unmasked!*, p. 143.

117. Quoted in Graham, *Current Biography Yearbook, 1996*, p. 77.

118. Quoted in Trakin, *Jim Carrey Unmasked!*, p. 151.

119. Quoted in Trakin, *Jim Carrey Unmasked!*, p. 153.

120. Quoted in Siegel, *The Jim Carrey Scrapbook*, p. 90.

121. Quoted in Trakin, *Jim Carrey Unmasked!*, p. 156.

122. Quoted in Trakin, *Jim Carrey Unmasked!*, p. 154.

123. Quoted in Trakin, *Jim Carrey Unmasked!*, p. 158.

124. Quoted in Handy, "Don't Laugh," p. 82.

125. Quoted in Trakin, *Jim Carrey Unmasked!*, pp. 150, 162–63.

126. Quoted in Trakin, *Jim Carrey Unmasked!*, p. 166.

127. Quoted in Siegel, *The Jim Carrey Scrapbook*, p. 84.

128. Quoted in Siegel, *The Jim Carrey Scrapbook*, p. 88.

129. Quoted in Harris, *Biography Today*, p. 44.

130. Quoted in Schruers, "Oh, Please Don't Do That," p. 125.

131. Quoted in Schruers, "Oh, Please Don't Do That," p. 125.

132. Quoted in Giles, "Funny Face," p. 50.

133. Quoted in Harris, *Biography Today*, p. 44.

134. Quoted in Josh Rottenberg, "Arrested Development," *Premiere,* March 1997, p. 100.

Chapter 6: "How Dare He Try to Do Something Different"

135. Quoted in Schruers, "Oh, Please Don't Do That," p. 72.

136. Quoted in Schruers, "Oh, Please Don't Do That," p. 72.

137. Quoted in Sherrill, "Renaissance Man," p. 100.

138. Quoted in Siegel, *The Jim Carrey Scrapbook*, p. 113.

139. Quoted in Sherrill, "Renaissance Man," p. 106.

140. Quoted in Schneider, "Doing Just Dandy," p. 3.

141. Quoted in Rottenberg, "Arrested Development," p. 66.

142. Quoted in Rottenberg, "Arrested Development," p. 66.

143. Quoted in Rottenberg, "Arrested Development," p. 68.

144. Quoted in Rottenberg, "Arrested Development," p. 66.

145. Quoted in Strauss, "Carrey on the Line," p. 1.

146. Quoted in Rottenberg, "Arrested Development," p. 64.

147. Quoted in Rottenberg, "Arrested Development," p. 64.

148. Quoted in Scott Collins, "*Liar, Liar* Team Comes Clean," *Newsday*, March 25, 1997, p. 1.

Chapter 7: "Fame Is What He Wanted, You Know"

149. Quoted in Collins, "*Liar, Liar* Team Comes Clean," p. 3.

150. Quoted in Smith, "Do Not Adjust Your Set," p. 27.

151. Quoted in Smith, "Do Not Adjust Your Set," p. 29.

152. Quoted in Handy, "Don't Laugh," p. 81.

153. Quoted in Judy Brennan, "Is Jim Carrey Flying in the Face of Success Again?" *Los Angeles Times*, April 9, 1997, p. 2.

154. Jonathan Palmer, "So What If Jim Carrey Wants to Switch Gears?" *Los Angeles Times*, April 19, 1997, p. 3.

155. Quoted in Sheila Johnston, "The Clevering-Up of America," *Independent*, September 20, 1998, p. 1.

156. Corliss, "Smile! Your Life's on TV," p. 78.

157. Quoted in Trakin, *Jim Carrey Unmasked!*, p. 150.

158. Quoted in Schruers, "Oh, Please Don't Do That," p. 125.

159. Quoted in Handy, "Don't Laugh," p. 80.

160. Quoted in Sherrill, "Renaissance Man," p. 102.

161. Quoted in Strauss, "Carrey on the Line," p. 2.

162. Quoted in Smith, "Do Not Adjust Your Set," p. 29.

163. Quoted in Smith, "Do Not Adjust Your Set," p. 29.

164. Quoted in Harris, *Biography Today*, p. 43.

165. Quoted in Collins and Speace, *Newsmakers,* p. 76.

166. Quoted in Trakin, *Jim Carrey Unmasked!*, p. 166.

167. Quoted in Rottenberg, "Arrested Development," p. 64.

168. Quoted in Trakin, *Jim Carrey Unmasked!*, pp. 161–62.

169. Quoted in Handy, "Don't Laugh," pp. 80–81.

170. Quoted in Trakin, *Jim Carrey Unmasked!*, p. 200.

171. Quoted in Strauss, "Carrey on the Line," p. 3.

172. Quoted in Siegel, *The Jim Carrey Scrapbook,* p. 113.

Important Dates in the Life of Jim Carrey

1962

James Eugene Carrey is born in Newmarket, Ontario, on January 17.

1975

Carrey's father loses his accounting job; the family works at Titan Wheels.

1977

Carrey is booed off the stage at Yuk Yuks in Toronto.

1978

Carrey drops out of school; the Carreys quit their factory jobs and are homeless.

1979

Carrey successfully returns to Yuk Yuks.

1981

Newspaper critic Bruce Blackadar heralds Carrey as a future star; Carrey heads to Los Angeles and begins performing at comedy clubs; he drops off the comedy club circuit to refashion his act.

1982

NBC signs Carrey to act in *The Duck Factory*.

1984

The Duck Factory starts its limited run on NBC; Carrey acts in his first movie, *Finders Keepers*.

1985

Carrey appears in *Once Bitten*.

1986
Carrey acts in *Peggy Sue Got Married;* he weds Melissa Wormer on March 28.

1987
Daughter, Jane, is born.

1988
Carrey acts in *The Dead Pool.*

1989
Carrey acts in *Pink Cadillac;* he appears in *Earth Girls Are Easy* and meets Damon Wayans; he acts in an uncredited role in *High Strung,* a movie that is released in 1994.

1990
In Living Color debuts on television and gives Carrey his first national exposure.

1991
Carrey tapes his Showtime cable special, *Jim Carrey's Unnatural Act;* his mother dies of kidney failure.

1992
Carrey wins acclaim with his dramatic performance in the television movie *Doing Time on Maple Drive.*

1994
Carrey stars in three blockbuster films in a row, *Ace Ventura: Pet Detective, The Mask,* and *Dumb and Dumber;* his father dies from cancer.

1995
Carrey divorces Melissa Wormer; he stars in *Batman Forever* and *Ace Ventura: When Nature Calls.*

1996
Carrey marries actress Lauren Holly; he stars in *The Cable Guy.*

1997
Carrey stars in *Liar, Liar.*

1998
Carrey stars in *The Truman Show* and *Simon Birch;* he completes filming of *Man on the Moon.*

1999
Carrey wins a Golden Globe for his role in *The Truman Show.*

For Further Reading

Judy Brennan, "Is Jim Carrey Flying in the Face of Success Again?" *Los Angeles Times,* April 9, 1997. Presents Carrey's dilemma of attempting the serious role in *The Truman Show.*

Business Wire, "Jim Carrey to Be MGM's *Fool on the Hill,*" October 29, 1997. Reports Carrey's acceptance of a role in the movie *Fool on the Hill.*

Celeb Web Site, "Jim Carrey," 1998. A useful summary of Carrey's career, with links to other sites. www.celebsite.com.

Scott Collins, "*Liar, Liar* Team Comes Clean," *Newsday,* March 25, 1997. A wide-ranging interview with Carrey that includes his thoughts for the future.

Paula Guzzetti, *Jim Carrey.* Parsippany, NJ: Dillon Press, 1998. A biography written for upper elementary school students.

Mary Hughes, *Jim Carrey.* Philadelphia: Chelsea House, 1999. A recent biography written for the junior high school market.

Dan Santow and Marie Moneysmith, "Love with the Proper Costar," *People,* September 5, 1994. Details how Carrey met Lauren Holly.

Jeff Strickler, "Call of the Wildman," *Star Tribune,* November 10, 1995. A helpful summary of Carrey's *Ace Ventura: When Nature Calls.*

Time, "World's Only Living Toon," August 8, 1994. Includes some useful material about his film *The Mask.*

United Press International, "Carrey Back on Set After Injury,"

September 23, 1998. Contains quotes from Carrey's camp following his incident in the ring during *Man on the Moon*.

Joan Wallner, *Jim Carrey: Funny Man*. Edina, MN: Abdo & Daughters, 1996. A brief biography written for elementary school students.

Works Consulted

Bridget Byrne, "*In Living Color*'s Funny Face Plays It Straight," *TV Guide*, March 14, 1992. An examination of Carrey's decision to accept his serious role in *Doing Time on Maple Drive*.

Louise Mooney Collins and Geri J. Speace, eds., *Newsmakers: The People Behind Today's Headlines*. Detroit: Gale Research, 1995. Concise look at Carrey's rapid rise to stardom.

Scott Collins, "*Liar, Liar* Team Comes Clean," *Newsday*, March 25, 1997. An interview with Carrey that examines his work in *Liar, Liar* and other films.

Richard Corliss, "Smile! Your Life's on TV," *Time*, June 1, 1998. A thorough analysis of Carrey's work in *The Truman Show* and of the importance of the movie.

Jeff Giles, "Funny Face," *Newsweek*, June 26, 1995. A helpful summary of Carrey's emergence to stardom that focuses on his early hits.

Judith Graham, ed., *Current Biography Yearbook, 1996*. New York: H. W. Wilson, 1996. A comprehensive examination of Carrey's start in entertainment, based on current periodicals and interviews.

Kendall Hamilton, "Not Another Pretty Face," *Newsweek*, July 25, 1994. Decent summary of Carrey's life written as he completed *Dumb and Dumber*.

Bruce Handy, "Don't Laugh," *Time*, June 1, 1998. A helpful examination of Carrey after completing *The Truman Show*.

Laurie Lanzen Harris, ed., *Biography Today*. Detroit: Omnigraphics,

1998. A valuable summary of Jim Carrey's life, as well as the lives of other notable individuals.

"Jim Carrey: The Joker's Wild," *A & E's Biography*, 1997. A balanced video presentation of Carrey's life that includes interviews with family and friends.

Sheila Johnston, "The Clevering-Up of America," *Independent*, September 20, 1998. An excellent look at Carrey and *The Truman Show*.

Jonathan Palmer, "So What If Jim Carrey Wants to Switch Gears?" *Los Angeles Times*, April 19, 1997. A favorable analysis of Carrey's desire to act in serious roles.

Josh Rottenberg, "Arrested Development," *Premiere*, March 1997. An insightful article focusing on Carrey's career in the 1990s, including some enlightening quotes.

Karen S. Schneider, "Doing Just Dandy: Fame Offers Jim Carrey the First Dance—and the Last Laugh," *People*, June 24, 1996. A useful look at Carrey's background.

Fred Schruers, "Oh, Please Don't Do That," *Rolling Stone*, July 13–27, 1995. An in-depth article containing excellent material on Carrey's youth, early years, and work in *Batman Forever*.

Andy Seiler, "Private Ryan Conquers Globes," *USA Today*, January 25, 1999. A summary of the Golden Globe award ceremony, at which Carrey had the audience in stitches.

Martha Sherrill, "Renaissance Man," *Esquire*, December 1995. A decent summary of Carrey's recent roles and his influence on the industry.

Scott and Barbara Siegel, eds., *The Jim Carrey Scrapbook*. New York: Citadel Press, 1995. A helpful collection of photographs and text that covers Carrey's family life, start in entertainment, and Hollywood career.

Chris Smith, "Do Not Adjust Your Set," *New York*, June 1, 1998. A superb analysis of Carrey's career in the months immediately prior to *The Truman Show*.

Bob Strauss, "Carrey on the Line," *Star Tribune,* June 14, 1996. A readable summary of Carrey's career that contains excellent comments from the star.

Roy Trakin, *Jim Carrey Unmasked!* New York: St. Martin's, 1995. A superb biography written by a veteran Hollywood observer; includes much useful information on every phase of Carrey's life.

Index

Picture Credits

Cover photo: Photofest

AP/Wide World Photos, 32

Archive Photos, 11, 67, 81

Archive Photos/Fotos International, 25, 65, 79 (bottom)

Corbis, 29

Corbis-Bettmann, 21

Corbis/Mitchell Gerber, 42, 48

Corbis/Kurt Kreiger, 36

Corbis/Neal Preston, 53

Lee/Archive Newsphotos, 62

© Pacha/Corbis, 86

PhotoDisc, 30

Photofest, 13, 14, 18, 35, 39, 40, 44, 46, 47, 52, 55, 59, 64, 66, 68, 70, 74, 76, 79 (top), 85, 89

Reuters/Fred Prouser/Archive Photos, 71

© Marko Shark/Corbis, 16

About the Author

John F. Wukovits is a junior high school teacher and writer from Trenton, Michigan, who specializes in history and biography. He has written biographies of Anne Frank, Martin Luther King Jr., Stephen King, Admiral Clifton Sprague, Barry Sanders, Tim Allen, Jack Nicklaus, Vince Lombardi, and Wyatt Earp. A graduate of the University of Notre Dame, Wukovits is the father of three daughters—Amy, Julie, and Karen.